THE SHAPING OF PROTESTANT EDUCATION

Monographs in Christian Education

C. ELLIS NELSON, *Editor*

THE SHAPING

OF PROTESTANT

EDUCATION

An Interpretation
of the Sunday School and the Development
of Protestant Educational Strategy
in the United States, 1789-1860

by WILLIAM BEAN KENNEDY

ASSOCIATION PRESS, NEW YORK

THE SHAPING OF PROTESTANT EDUCATION

Publisher's stock number: 1610
Library of Congress catalog card number: 66-15749

PRINTED IN THE UNITED STATES OF AMERICA

INTRODUCTION

Protestantism's overall educational effort involves its alliance with general education and the institutions and agencies under its control. These divisions overlap and interpenetrate each other as they form the Protestant strategy in education. The word "strategy" suggests that Protestants have a self-conscious, articulate conception of what they want in their religious education and that they have devised means of getting it. Rather, what we now have in Protestantism reveals the haphazard historical development of Protestant educational efforts. We have many theories in religious education; we have given careful consideration to the relation of Protestant belief to the social sciences, especially psychology, but we have paid scant attention to the institutions, agencies, and structures by which we transmit our faith.

The problems of Protestants as they struggle to adapt themselves to a public school system with an increasingly secular orientation and a neutrality toward religious teachings and ceremonies have been discussed by Dr. Robert W. Lynn in the first monograph in this series, *Protestant Strategies in Education.*

In this essay Dr. William B. Kennedy gives us the background for facing our church-sponsored educational program. By examining the period prior to the Civil War when Protestant patterns of education were formed, Dr. Kennedy is able to show how the Sunday school in some areas served both the function of public school and the purposes of the church; how the church, when it became aware of the results of the legal separation from public education, attempted in some places to set up a parochial school system; and how the Sunday school was finally adopted by the denominations as their principal educational agency. Thus we have inherited an educational agency that served the churches' needs when the United States was rural, Protestant, agrarian, and dominated by an expanding western frontier mentality.

Today we live in an urban, technical society. Except in a few isolated communities, the Protestant ethos has been replaced by a pluralistic spirit created by the existence of various religious communities and a large body of citizens who have no formal religious commitment. Can the units of the church school, of which the Sunday school remains the most widespread, be our major Protestant effort? To answer that question we have first to know what the Sunday school was, how it claimed the attention of the church, how it transcended denominational boundaries, why it depended on lay leadership and emphasized evangelistic activity. The better we understand the formation of our churches' educational strategy and the Sunday school as an agency of that strategy, the freer we will be to open afresh the problem in its contemporary setting and move to new solutions that would serve the millions of children, youth, and adults who depend upon the church for religious instruction.

—C. ELLIS NELSON
Editor, Monographs in Christian Education

CONTENTS

PREFACE

Protestant education as we know it in America took shape during the National Period, from 1789 to 1860. During those years there arose the common schools, public institutions of higher learning, and church agencies of education such as the Sunday school and the denominational colleges and seminaries. Today, however, conditions have changed radically from those in which these institutions emerged. As religious educators ask anew the basic questions about how the church can effectively educate, they need insight into how its present patterns of schooling developed in that nineteenth century historical context.

But where can one gain such insight? Histories of general education describe the rise of church colleges and mention the Sunday school, as do histories of the American church, but neither provide adequate interpretation. Most histories of religious education in America do not analyze the Sunday school in a sufficiently broad context. Those that attempt to do so show their age and reflect the propagandistic approach of most historical writing of fifty years ago. What is needed is a study which traces the developing educational strategy of the Protestant church in the new United States, and particularly the major agency of the Sunday school, during those early decades when that strategy was taking shape alongside the two more massive structures to which it inevitably related, the public school and the denominational church.

Because the fields of educational and church history are both in flux today,[1] the author found himself exploring both fields in some detail as he undertook this study, in order to place the Sunday school in right perspective. The author does not claim to be a specialist in the history either of American education or of American religious life, although his background of interest and training has included both. Specialists in both those fields will recognize limitations in his total grasp, but hopefully they will profit from the attempt to relate the two fields to each other and to the middle agency, the Sunday school. Helpful guidance came from Lawrence A. Cremin in the field of educational history and from Robert T. Handy and James H. Smylie in American church history. Many others have contributed to the study through conversation, correspondence, and criticism. The author's gratitude goes also to the administration and faculty of Union Theological Seminary in Virginia for a year of sabbatical study; to the American Association of Theological Schools for a grant to pursue this research; and to Union Theological Seminary in New York City for providing visiting scholar privileges during the period of study.

The notes include guidance to the major literature used for the important issues; citations there are not repeated in the bibliography, which lists only those primary and secondary sources that were vital in providing major understanding of the Sunday school and its development. The reader who desires to check on interpretations or to pursue further his own study beyond what has been done here, hopefully will find these references useful. Those who do discover serious omissions or errors in citations or analysis are encouraged to correspond with the author, so that the efforts of both may contribute to deeper understanding of a complex problem.

In the light of the evidence, it is possible to affirm that the major issues of church educational strategy were faced and discussed and that broad solutions were reached by American Protestantism by the Civil War. The thesis here is that during the period from 1789 to 1860 American Protestantism adopted a general strategy of education that depended heavily upon the public school and alongside it utilized the Sunday school as the major church-related instrument for Christian education.

PROLOGUE: *The Development of the American Sunday School 1789-1860*

In the New World the colonists established schools like those they had known back home. Because education had been strongly religious there, the church either controlled or heavily influenced its processes in the colonies. In the unsettled conditions in America, however, the desire for education produced many different types of schools. Groups of citizens, local governing bodies, or clergymen tried to provide instruction. Where the church was weak or lacked trained clergymen (as it usually did in those days), schooling was difficult to sustain. Furthermore, the demanding activities of colonial settlement limited leisure time so that the general level of education tended to be low. British missionaries stressed the discouraging state of culture when they appealed for funds, and colonial leaders often shared their concern. Despite the obstacles, however, colonial Americans struggled to maintain schools.

Because education and religion were closely tied, the changing character of church life affected the schools. As cycles of decline and revival appeared in the eighteenth century, the stable parish tended to give way before the mobility and scattering which fostered free church organizations. For a person to be born into the established church was becoming less important than for him to make a voluntary decision to belong. Persuasion succeeded coercion as the major means of gettin⌐

active involvement. The strong emphasis on evangelism came to influence all the customary activities of church life, including education.

Further educational decline came with the Revolution, and the early problems of independence left people little energy for formal schooling. The shock of losing state support affected seriously those churches that had formerly enjoyed establishment, and all religious groups had to adjust to the new conditions. Inevitably the schools related to churches were affected too. General education, for centuries largely under the influence of the church, now had to develop other forms that did not depend on the old ecclesiastical structures. The emergence of common schools, colleges, and the Sunday school in the National Period all exemplify that development.

The early Sunday schools in America offered general education to poor children, as had their models in England. Usually organized groups of benevolent citizens formed schools, first in eastern seaboard cities, with two predominant aims. They wanted to bring the children and young people to Christ, and they wanted to train them in the three "R's" and Christian morality so that they would be safe and useful citizens. These schools, held on Sunday usually, were related to churches, and the children often attended worship as a body. At first, however, they were not in any direct sense church schools. Gradually from such "sporadic beginnings" the Sunday school began to emerge as an important agency of education.[1]

By 1824 enough local societies existed for a national organization to be formed. Called the American Sunday School Union, it followed the pattern of other benevolent societies, particularly the American Bible Society founded in 1816. The ASSU dominated the early decades of the Sunday school movement. Its title indicated its nature: *American* suggested its contribution to the growing national consciousness; *Sunday*

School was its program emphasis, although it also published religious books and lesson materials; and, because it included persons from different denominations, it proudly used the word *Union*.[2]

Largely a lay affair, the ASSU held its annual meeting in Philadelphia, often just after the meetings of other societies in New York, and concurrently with the Presbyterian General Assembly. Benevolent gifts furnished the major means of support, although sales of books brought in some income with more or less regularity. Because of communication and organizational difficulties, and despite vigorous efforts, the ASSU could not maintain any effective control over local Sunday schools or provide accurate reports on the national Sunday school movement.

Nevertheless the ASSU shared the excitement and momentum of the benevolent crusade as it flourished during the 1820's and 1830's. Working with the westward expansion of the country, the Union launched in 1830 a major drive to "ESTABLISH A SUNDAY-SCHOOL IN EVERY DESTITUTE PLACE WHERE IT IS PRACTICABLE, THROUGHOUT THE VALLEY OF THE MISSISSIPPI."[3] Within two years New York had contributed nearly $18,000 to the campaign, Pennsylvania over $10,000, and seven other states over $2,000 each. The drive established hundreds of schools in the West. In many places these schools served as the first formal organization for either educational or religious purposes.

At first directed toward unchurched children, the Sunday schools soon enrolled children of church members as well. As part of the evangelical movement, they sought to bring the children to conversion. Their teachers were volunteers, frequently not much older than their scholars, and they studied materials produced by the Sunday school societies.[4]

As the denominations became more self-conscious, however, they wanted to control their own Sunday schools. Beginning in 1825 they began to form their own societies which organized Sunday schools and produced denominational lesson materials. By 1860 the union Sunday school movement had given way in large measure to Sunday schools under church, i.e., denominational, control. The great thrust of union effort had made its contribution. In becoming church-controlled the Sunday school shared the general movement toward denominationalism in American church life.

During these same decades the common schools were coming into being. As they offered general education on weekdays, the less efficient schools on Sunday lost that function. Furthermore, the new common schools included Bible and moral teaching, since they reflected the common Protestant atmosphere of the society. As they expanded, they quickly became the major institution in a dual pattern of education in America. Alongside the general moral teaching of the common schools, the Sunday schools were supposed to emphasize the particular teachings of the various denominations. Despite some misgivings, the large majority of Protestant churchmen and Sunday school leaders supported this parallel pattern.

A few religious groups refused, however, and began to develop church-controlled weekday education in parochial schools. The Roman Catholics did so, aware of the predominant Protestantism of the public schools. So did other groups with high ethnic intensity and often a foreign language with which to hold out against the Americanizing and Protestantizing influences of the common schools. After a serious effort at private schooling, the Presbyterians gave it up and joined their fellow Protestants in support of the dual pattern of common schools and church Sunday schools.

As the denominations took over the Sunday schools, they

were utilizing a new agency that had originated outside the church. This new agency had to be related to educational practices such as catechetical training, confirmation classes, and other occasions when the minister taught. It needed to be brought more directly into relationship with the central structures of church life. Its lay character, its emphasis upon children, its evangelistic rather than nurture emphasis, and its lack of continuity with the denominational heritages made its assimilation difficult.

Despite these developments and problems, however, the Sunday school grew and prospered, and made significant contributions to American educational and church life in those decades. As the Protestant churches of America established themselves firmly in the new nation under radically new structures of separation of church and state, they influenced strongly the course of American life, and, in so doing, contributed to Christendom and the world a most significant experiment in religious freedom. In that long story the American Sunday school, as it became the central agency of church education, played its part and made its contribution.

THE SHAPING OF PROTESTANT EDUCATION

1. THE RELATIONSHIP OF THE SUNDAY SCHOOL TO THE PUBLIC SCHOOL

Because of the major significance of public schools in American education, the relation of the Sunday Schools to their development assumes prime importance in interpreting the development of Protestant educational strategy. The Sunday school served first as forerunner to the common school, and then as its religious partner in a dual pattern.

Precursor and Pioneer

And in the less enlightened sections of our country, in many portions of the new States, and in many dark corners of our larger towns and cities, where vice and ignorance together congregate, the Sunday-school, by the self-denying labors of the missionary, with the aid of the even more unceasing and earnest philanthropist, the Sunday-school teacher, oftentimes becomes the precursor and pioneer both of the district school and of the church. In multitudes of instances it becomes both the moral and mental light of the neighborhood, and children and adults here learn to read who otherwise could not or would not do so.[1]

Thus did Henry Barnard's influential educational journal evaluate the place of the Sunday school in preceding and preparing for the common school. Given its English precedent, the American Sunday school naturally served as advance guard for the common school. The charity-school movement in Great Britain, of which the Sunday school was a part, succeeded in supplying "an interim organisation for semi-popular education until the State was ready to take up its duty. . . ." [2] In America the same claim can be made.

The early Sunday schools provided general elementary education. The "first-day societies" of New York and Philadelphia established schools open to the populace at large, especially to poor children with no other means of formal education.[3] For example, a Boston report in 1817, noting that children had to know how to read before entering town schools, affirmed the need for schooling from ages four to seven. "But until this is done," the report continued, "there is but one expedient to meet the exigencies of the case, and that is, the establishment of Sunday Schools. . . ." [4] While evangelism was a primary aim of Sunday schools, they performed a much broader task of general education. ASSU reports showed continuing concern over illiteracy statistics in the various states and encouraged Sunday schools to teach reading.

On the frontier, Sunday schools dramatically fulfilled this function. In the crude conditions of early settlement few forces worked to provide education. Particularly in the Mississippi Valley, but elsewhere as well, the Sunday schools often offered the only opportunities to learn to read and write. At least one Sunday school missionary, Stephen Paxson, received all his formal education in the Sunday school—a story he often told as he appealed for funds in the eastern cities.[5]

In other ways Sunday schools pioneered for public schools. They tried to bring order into society, seeking in the cities to influence "vicious youth" and others who threatened public order, and on the frontier to civilize the settlers. They also tried consciously to make of their pupils good American citizens. Patriotic fervor stands out in the literature of the Sunday school movement. In 1841 one of the most advertised books of the ASSU was a *Life of Washington.* Francis Scott Key was long a manager of the Union. Its annual reports sound as nationalistic as any patriotic journal, as in this rhapsodic sample of 1831:

> It would be worth all it costs were it only for its instrumentality in teaching children and adults to read,—but it has done more than this;—it has formed in them the prevailing habit of reading and thinking, and a taste for intellectual enjoyment. . . .
>
> It would be worth all it costs, were it only for the habits of cleanliness and subordination which it has produced wherever a school has been faithfully conducted;—but it has done more than this—it has produced habits of sobriety, temperance, and reverence for the Sabbath, and the countless blessings and enjoyments that for ever attend these virtues.
>
> It would be worth all it costs, were it only for the silent and insensible influence which it sheds upon society;—but it has done specific, visible, tangible service to the State. By means of it, the ignorant have been taught; the degraded have been elevated; enemies to each other have been reconciled; profligates have been reclaimed; drunkards have been reformed; infidels have been converted, and the thoughtless have been alarmed. By its influence, light has been brought out of darkness and order out of confusion; domestic peace has been established; the altar of domestic worship has been reared; the Sabbath has been consecrated; congregations have been gathered; churches of the living God have been planted, and in solitary places where no voice was, notes of joy and gladness, thanksgiving and the voice of melody are now heard.
>
> This is not a picture of fancy; every line has its bold original in the correspondence of the American Sunday School Union during the last twelve months. . . .[6]

The Sunday school helped prepare for the public school merely by existing. The presence of an organized school with

a building, books, teachers, and pupils helped make acceptable the idea of common school on weekdays. The union
schools sought broad support by local people in order to foster
community initiative and responsibility. The publications of
the Union were intended to serve beyond the narrowly religious
aim. An ASSU primer to teach reading sold one hundred
thousand copies between 1850 and 1854. Sunday school emphasis on libraries put collections of books in many places
where a public school or general library did not exist until
decades later. Through such activities the Union made considerable contributions to the education of the nation.

As common schools began to be organized,[7] Sunday school
men and clergymen were often leaders in the movement. In
Kentucky, Dr. Benjamin O. Peers was the first state school
superintendent, and seven of the first eight superintendents
were clergymen. The Rev. R. J. Breckenridge, long a leader in
the ASSU, vocal opponent of the Presbyterian parochial
school plan, and the sixth Superintendent of Public Instruction, was called "the framer and builder of the common school
system of Kentucky." [8] In New York, Pennsylvania, and even
more frequently in the West, the names of Sunday school
leaders appear in the lists of those working to establish public schools. The long-time president of the ASSU, Alexander
Henry, served on the Philadelphia School Board. Throughout
the Ohio Valley ministers connected with the ASSU and other
benevolent societies were prominent in early educational efforts.[9] Thus those connected with the Sunday school provided
significant support and leadership to the growing common
school movement.

However, all Sunday school leaders did not support the
public school development. The 1831 ASSU report includes
some passages where extravagant claims made for the Sunday
school seemed to pit it as a serious alternative to weekday

common schools. The new public school movement in Massachusetts, identified with Horace Mann, tended to reflect the more liberal and Unitarian elements in society, so that churchmen there who would ordinarily have been supporters did not participate as vigorously as might have been the case had the theological conflict not intruded. Generally, those Sunday school leaders who liked "Union schools" with little denominational distinctiveness found it easier to support public schools than those who wanted to emphasize particular "sectarian tenets." In regard to leaders in the Sunday school movement, the statement in *American Christianity* seems to be correct: "With a few exceptions, Protestants eagerly supported the expanding public schools, which were becoming more secular," and "contributed significantly to the development of the public school systems of elementary and secondary education." [10]

In significant ways, therefore, the Sunday school movement served as "precursor and pioneer" [11] to public schools in the United States. Just how strong a factor it was is hard to measure. Cubberley's estimate that the Sunday schools helped awaken an educational consciousness certainly seems true.[12] In fact, the Sunday school movement may deserve more credit than it has been given for its work as pioneer of the public schools. Beyond its general influence toward a broader educational system, the movement made the contributions of its publications, its organizations, and its leaders that need to be remembered. In serving as a valuable preparatory agency during the early decades of American national history, the Sunday school was both "precursor and pioneer" to the common schools.

In serving that function, however, the Sunday school inevitably seemed transitory. As long as the frontier kept moving westward and outward from the cities, it could exist helpfully as pioneer of weekday public education. But wherever the pioneering function persisted, the Sunday school tended to delay development of the more distinctively religious function that was to characterize its permanent relationship to the common schools.

Religious Partner

With the rise of public weekday schools, the Sunday school shifted toward a more specialized religious function. Note Barnard again:

> Religious instruction has been withdrawn from the common school and intrusted wholly to the home and the church; and as "the Evangelist of the district school," the Sunday-school has arisen, not indeed to interrupt or displace parental and pastoral culture but to supply their unavoidable deficiencies and to act where they can not. As improvements have been made and a rapid advancement effected in the system of free popular secular instruction, so a like progress is evident in the kindred system of popular religious culture, for the systems though distinct are not wholly independent, the two react mutually in a measure upon each other, as the one is the complement of the other.[13]

In his official report to the British government Edward Twisleton gave a similar analysis based on investigation of the New England schools and interviews with leading public figures such as Daniel Webster. He concluded:

> 1st. That the New England system of free schools is not sectarian in its tendencies;
> 2ndly. That it is not irreligious;
> 3rdly. That, indirectly, at least, if not directly, it is religious, in the sense of being favourable to the cultivation of the religious sentiments and to the promotion of morality;
> 4thly. That by means of Sunday schools, combined with the teaching of parents at home and instruction from the pulpit in Church, the children of the free schools are, for the most part,

taught the peculiar tenets of the various religious denominations to which they respectively belong.

5thly. That the system of free schools in New England is effective in giving instruction to the children of the poorest classes, and is deserving of approbation.[14]

By 1860 there had emerged a general consensus in American Protestantism that the combination of public and Sunday school teaching would largely take care of the needed religious teaching of the young. In that pattern the public school was primary; the Sunday school was adjunct to it, providing the specific religious teaching it could not include. Only on the basis of such widespread Protestant dependence upon common schools for a fundamental part of religious education can the place of the Sunday school be understood.

Except for infrequent grandiose claims, contemporary commentators admitted that the Sunday school alone could not carry the burden of religious teaching. In 1838 an Episcopal educator wrote that he felt "constrained to regard it in the light of a temporary and most inadequate expedient." [15] He argued that it embraced a very small proportion of the children of the country, its teachers were generally incompetent, and it commanded too small an amount of time each week. Others made the same points.[16] By 1860 few claimed that the Sunday school could carry out the religious and moral teaching required for the children of the nation. Admittedly the public school had to do part of it.

Common school leaders were quite willing to assume the responsibility. Horace Mann protested vigorously against criticism that the schools in Massachusetts did not teach religion. He cited the law of 1789, repeated in 1827, which enjoined common school instructors

. . . to take diligent care and exert their best endeavors to impress on the minds of children and youth committed to their care and instruction, the principles of piety, justice and a sacred regard to truth, love to their country, humanity and universal benevolence, sobriety, industry, frugality, chastity, moderation and temperance, and those other virtues which are the ornament of human society and the basis upon which the republican Constitution is structured . . .[17]

In his diary on January 20, 1839, Mann wrote: "The fundamental principles of Christianity may and should be inculcated [in the common schools]. . . . After this, each denomination must be left to its own resources, for inculcating its own faith or creed." [18]

However, between "not sectarian" and "not irreligious" lay a morass of confusion and controversy. In one way or another almost everyone expected the public schools to be religious. But defining the content of the religious instruction proved to be difficult. One of Twisleton's correspondents had written that "religion is not taught as a matter of theology, according to the forms of the Catechism, but is generally inculcated as a matter of devotion and of Christian morals. The Scriptures are almost universally used in some way in the public schools." [19] In most places the schools began by teaching the predominant religious beliefs of the community, particularly where there was religious homogeneity. But objections soon led to the difficulty of finding much doctrine that would be acceptable to all. The tendency was to rule out anything not believed in common. Horace Mann prescribed general "principles of piety." Thus "sectarian religion" was kept out and moral and religious teachings were kept in the curriculum.

In practice such criteria led to two major results. There was general agreement on the importance of reading the Bible in the public schools. Mann proudly cited the use of the Bible in the schools of Massachusetts, and noted that the board required it in the normal schools. Actually the Bible furnished almost the only basis upon which Protestant sectarian groups could cooperate. Calvin E. Stowe proclaimed the prevailing attitude before the American Institute of Instruction in 1844: "Let not infidel coldness, jesuitical intolerance, or sectarian jealousy, rob our schools of their greatest ornament and most precious treasure, the Bible of our fathers." [20]

A second result was to stress morality rather than doctrine. Already the revivals had contributed to a simplification of Christian doctrine, so that a conversion experience and a moral life had become the significant marks of faith. Whatever their theological creeds, most Americans believed in morality for the good of the nation. Although many protested that ethics could not so easily be cut loose from theology, the pragmatic tendency was to do so, and to stress moral teaching. Sherman M. Smith states that "morality and ethics had come by 1837 to replace practically all the definitely religious content in the textbooks." [21]

The schoolbooks of the period show the heavy emphasis upon religion and morality. Henry Steele Commager was correct in commenting that the morality of the McGuffey readers (of which over one hundred million were sold between 1836 and 1890)

> was deeply religious, and in those mid-century years, in America, religion meant Protestant Christianity. . . . The world of the McGuffeys was a world where no one questioned the truths of the Bible, or their relevance to every-day conduct, and where the notion that the separation of church and state required the exclusion of religion from the schoolroom or from schoolbooks seemed preposterous.[22]

The American child during these years was taught a code of morality based upon Scripture, more or less derived from the common tradition which most Americans shared, and reflecting the predominant religious atmosphere.[23]

Protestants supported public schools because they saw them as a means for moral and spiritual instruction. They were conscious of the values of literacy and citizenship training, but for them the key was moral education. They expected basically a continuation of what they knew to have been the case for centuries: the schools in Western Christendom taught Christianity because it was a fundamental part of the society to which they belonged. The fact that a legal change had taken place had not at all convinced them that any radical change should take place in their local schools. The shift from establishment and coercion to moral suasion still allowed freedom to inculcate the faith as society's leaders saw it in the schools they built and operated. In many places legislation required Bible reading and prayer. In other places such practices were so universally assumed that they needed no legislative sanction. Generally public schoolteachers also reflected the predominant Protestant piety. Only as the Roman Catholic minority became significantly large in the eastern cities (after 1840) were Protestant leaders forced to reassess their assumptions about the effect of freedom of religion and religious pluralism on education.

Thus, with some misgivings but with general approval, the public schools undertook to teach morality, by means of Bible reading and ethical instruction. The Protestant churches were here committing an educational task that historically had been theirs to the governments of states and localities. The Erastian implications of that commitment were not clear even to those whose traditions were most un-Erastian. Why? Was it not because the Protestant citizenry assumed that the schools of the society would reflect its prevailing religion? In large measure their assumption proved correct. Their intuitive grasp of the situation resulted in a strategy dependence upon the public schools for common religious teaching that would continue for more than a century. In supporting the public schools Protestantism established the major framework for its educational strategy in America.

Alongside the common schools, in the "dual pattern," the Sunday school and other church programs would teach the particular "sectarian tenets" considered essential by the various denominations. In that light the content of Sunday school lessons needs to be re-evaluated.

In the early years of the century catechisms and other sectarian materials had been common textbooks in parish instruction. As the Sunday school arose, its goal of evangelizing children led to an emphasis on the Bible and the common items of Christian belief that were useful in preparing one for conversion. Unregulated memorization of Bible verses drew heavy criticism which exposed the need for better pedagogy and more organized curricula. The next stage, using selected passages and Scripture questions in hopes of deepening the study of the Bible, characterized the Sunday schools of the denominations as well as those of the ASSU.

But by 1840, the commencement of what Frank G. Lankard tabbed the "Babel period" of Sunday school curriculum history,[24] two new factors had emerged. The primary one was the rise of the common schools with their emphasis on Bible and moral teaching. In that context the Sunday school, the "evangelist of the district school," tried to teach much the same thing to the children and young people, adding a direct appeal for conversion. The other factor was the growing movement of denominational Sunday schools, to which the formation of denominational educational and publishing agencies attested. As public schools taught only "common Christianity," in the eyes of many churchmen denominational instruction became more and more important. Their attempts to control the Sunday schools in their churches and to provide curriculum materials fitted into the evolving strategy pattern in which Sunday schools would supplement with specific sectarian teaching what the children received in common schools. As the latter pre-empted the teaching of "common Christianity," however, the utility of union Sunday schools declined. Caught between a more massive and effective system of weekday education, which stressed the Bible and general Christian morality, and denominational Sunday schools, which sought to inculcate their own dogmatic teaching, the union schools had nowhere to go.

"Babel" therefore describes the period from only one point of view. Actually the variety of curriculum experiments illustrated the high creativity of an important stage in the determination of strategy. During these years the emerging denominational Sunday school organizations were searching for curriculum materials that would fortify the Sunday school at a point of great need—the inculcation of denominational beliefs and the nurture of their own children and young people.

In programs and teaching materials the common school and the Sunday school by 1860 were supplementary parts of the system by which American children and young people were educated. The two were seen together as great leveling institutions of society. Each contributed to the other. The common school served as the "nursery of the church," as Horace Bushnell described it, teaching church children and others how to read and to develop the skills for their future citizenship and religious life. By teaching morality and Bible, the day school served, in Horace Mann's words, as a "powerful auxiliary" to religious education. Because of the instruction given in Sunday school, the public school needed to provide only elementary religious teaching. On that basis it could fulfill its great aim as a *common* school—to provide the common American teaching and experience that would help produce mature citizens and a stable body politic in ensuing generations. The arrangement seemed admirable. No wonder the "eminent New Englanders" could boast about it to a visiting Britisher.

In fact there were those willing to go further. At least one state, Delaware, gave state subsidy to Sunday schools in recognition of their valuable part in the total work of education.[25] *The Common School Journal* of 1839 reported a meeting in New England where serious proposals were made to have Sunday school records of attainment transmitted to the public school, so that the educational transcript of each student could be complete. In most places no such specific relationship existed, but the two agencies were considered to be part of the one American system of education.

Sunday school leaders saw the two as related, but noted important dissimilarities. They admitted the obvious difference in the amount of class time. They explained the fact that their teachers were largely untrained by admitting the problem, but claiming several advantages also. With more teachers available, classes could be smaller, and the teacher could know his pupils more intimately, thereby influencing the children by his character. And, since the Sunday school stressed knowledge of God more than just knowledge, it valued the piety of the teacher highly.

However the need for simple lesson helps for teachers, and the difficulty of finding those equipped to use lesson materials effectively, gave further indication of the problem the Sunday school had with teachers. The problem was particularly obvious when the Sunday school's teachers were compared with the increasingly trained ones of the common schools. These characteristics showed the Sunday school to be standing midway between the home and the public school, less school-like than the latter but more so than the former, more intimate in its relationships than the latter but less so than the former; and as such it attempted to fulfill some of the inadequacies of both.

Effects of the Dual Pattern

The dual pattern affected the Sunday school in several ways. First, the pattern established the Sunday school firmly in the American structure of education. Instead of being completely superseded by the weekday common school, the Sunday school shifted from its original purpose to fulfill a specialized role in the total process of education.

Second, the pattern helped bring the Sunday schools under the control of the major institutional expressions of American church life, the denominations. The early interdenominational enthusiasm and lay leadership found itself now involved in a specialized task requiring close cooperation with the guardians of denominational traditions, the clergy and official church governing bodies. Although the cooperative endeavor was to be maintained in various forms thereafter, the rise of denominational boards indicated that the new pattern left little place for the union Sunday schools of the earlier period. The later significant contribution of the American Sunday school to ecumenical cooperation and thinking had to be made largely within the context of the predominant denominational mold of Protestant church life.

Third, the pattern helped stamp upon the Sunday school certain characteristics that, in the long run, were to prove troublesome. The system ascribed primary place to the public school. The Sunday school was its adjunct, supplementing it rather than standing alone. In this respect the Catholic decision to attempt parochial schools was more consistent with, and more dignifying to, the religious educational effort. As adjunct to the common schools, the Sunday schools thereafter were to be strongly influenced by them in many, many ways. Some of the influences were salutary, for instance, the continual challenge to match public school quality in facilities, textbooks, and teacher training. Others were threats. Since the aim of the public school and its basic operational philosophy did not come specifically from the Christian faith, imitation could be harmful to the church's schools. Furthermore, the Sunday school was part-time, radically so when compared to the full work week and the gradually lengthening public school year. It was therefore difficult to communicate a sense of the importance of the Sunday school's teaching when, to the pupils, it looked marginal to the major school effort. The Sunday school was by definition "sacred," since it was assigned that specialty. Common schools taught life, "real life," and prepared one to make a living and be a citizen in the republic. Sunday schools taught religion, and their institutional separation helped keep religion isolated from the major affairs of life. Thus the separated emphasis on the sacred led to an irrelevance that often relegated to the Sunday school a teaching of piety uninvolved with much of the mainstream of life. These characteristics did not have to lead to negative results, but the fact of institutional separation tended to push the Sunday school in these directions.

At the same time the pattern had an effect on the common schools. By assuming a major part of the moral and religious instruction of the American public, the schools took on a responsibility which they could not easily fulfill. Hence the long search for a workable program in this area of curriculum.[26] Hence also the emergence of a kind of Americanized religion in which a national morality and a "lowest-common-denominator" theology were mixed. In its pluralism the nation seemed to be seeking a kind of secularized faith that would give it "religious" foundation and continuity without the divisive and distinctive traditions of the various sects. In that search the public school was the laboratory for experimentation. Committed to teaching morality and a common religion, the schools began to assume some of the ecclesiastical atmosphere that went with the responsibility.

The former clear, legal union of church and state had been abandoned; now there was growing up a vague, new kind of tie in which a new kind of "church" was fostering a new kind of nationalized religion. The strong "social establishment" of predominant Protestantism was reflected in the institutions that tried to induct new generations of Americans into the meaning of life in the Republic. Bishop Hughes of New York saw the development as threatening to the Catholic church and criticized strongly what he called the "private, clandestine, surreptitious 'union of Church and State'" in public education.[27] Sidney E. Mead states the issue clearly when he says:

> . . . of necessity the state in its public-education system is and always has been teaching religion. It does so because the well-being of the nation and the state demands this foundation of shared beliefs. In other words, the public schools in the United States took over one of the basic responsibilities that traditionally was always assumed by an established church. In this sense the public-school system of the United States is its established church.[28]

The very success of the Protestant crusade [29] made it easy to assume that the dual system would work. As Winthrop S. Hudson points out, "The ideals, the convictions, the language, the customs, the institutions of society were so shot through with Christian presuppositions that the culture itself nurtured and nourished the Christian faith." [30] Although there were many other formal and informal agencies for that nurturing process, the public school became a primary one. In allowing

it to become central, the churches were in the long run risking
a great deal. As Hudson goes on to say:

> For the strength and vigor of the culture which the churches had
> brought into being led men to discount the importance of the
> churches and to neglect the springs from which the power and
> vitality of the culture had been derived. While faith could be
> nurtured by the culture apart from the churches, the Christian
> character of the culture could not be maintained apart from the
> churches.[31]

The separation of the public schools from the church's Sunday
schools contributed to that problem.

Nor can the broader implications for religion in the nation
be overlooked. For a millennium and a half religion in Western Christendom had been organized under the control and
guidance of ecclesiastical structures, the forms of order; continuity, and control of which rested largely in the hands of the
clergy. In the new American nation a part of religious expression in a significant institution for a very important segment of
the population was shifting to the control of the state, constitutionally separate from the churches. Various expedient ties
remained, one of which was quite obvious in regard to moral
and religious instruction. But the shift implied a much more
radical restructuring, not only of education, but also of the
understanding of religion itself and of its place in a pluralistic
society. The early Sunday schools had already begun to develop a "common Christianity," and under another form the
common schools took up the development. With the primary
assignment of responsibility given to the public schools, their
work would have immense effect upon the understanding of
religion gradually absorbed by Americans. The common
schools became an agency for the new religious identity of
Americans. Religion was tied to nationalism in a very subtle
and close way, and the Bible became a patriotic as well as a

religious symbol. The large majority of Christian people in America evidently were quite content to have it so.

*   *   *

In their relationship to common schools the American Sunday schools historically fulfilled two roles. They first were predecessors until the more effective weekday public schools could be established. Then they were supplementary, adjunct agencies charged with the special religious teaching desired by the dominant religious bodies in America. American Protestantism accepted the strategy pattern of education thus described, called by James Hastings Nichols the "dual pattern" of "parallel institutions . . . designed to educate children in secular and religious subjects respectively." [32] For over a century that pattern has provided the framework within which the Protestant churches have attempted to work out their particular programs of religious education. From time to time additional programs have been established and old ones modified. But since 1860 there has been no major challenge to that fundamental commitment. Any basic changes therefore must begin with an understanding of the fact of and the factors involved in the commitment to the dual pattern.

2. THE RELATIONSHIP OF THE SUNDAY SCHOOL TO THE CHURCH

In addition to its involvement with the emerging common schools, Protestant educational strategy was shaped as the Sunday school related to the developing forms of denominationalism. Here also it served first as pioneer or nursery, and then as an established institution permanently tied to the church.

Pioneer for the Church

As one of the benevolent societies of the evangelical movement the Sunday school shared the outreach atmosphere of the period. In many places it became an evangelistic agency for the church. During its early years, when the ASSU predominated, the Sunday school proudly claimed that it pioneered for the church where formal ecclesiastical organization was lacking. In many frontier settlements it enabled Christian and other leaders to unite in providing schooling for their children. As these pioneers organized Sunday schools, they prepared individuals for conversion when the time of revival came, and at the same time formed communities ready for the preachers who would bring persons into the church. In doing this the Sunday school was not a church; it served as pioneer for the church.

Around 1845 Frederick A. Packard of the ASSU estimated that probably a half or three fourths of the Sunday schools in the West and Southwest "were formed and are still held where there are no houses of worship." [1] In frontier areas the pioneering function served well, as Packard's description indicates:

> In some of the settlements where such labours as we have described are bestowed, the preaching of the Gospel is seldom or never enjoyed. In many it is enjoyed at intervals of some weeks, but not very regularly. Hence the Sabbath becomes an idle day, or is spent in secular labour, vain amusements, or vicious indulgences, so that the missionary finds the children are glad of the excitement, and are at once interested in the proceedings of the Sunday-school. Parents readily accompany their children to the place of meeting, and thus associate under good influences. The religious exercises of the school are easily expanded or prolonged to meet some of the religious wants of the parents and neighbours; and thus habits are formed which finally result in the call for the introduction of regular gospel institutions. The school-house is transformed into a place of public worship; the Sunday-school becomes the nucleus of a Christian church and congregation; and, in due time, a minister of the gospel is permanently established among them. This is no visionary sketch, but has been substantially realized in hundreds upon hundreds of instances, by the missionaries of the American Sunday School Union. [2]

Once the church was organized, the function of the Sunday school shifted somewhat. Now children of church members attended along with others, and they came into full church membership through the school. In fact, the Sunday school often became the chief channel by which new members came. The logic was clear:

It is felt that, if there is any good reason for each denomination to have its distinctive churches, there is an equally good reason for having its distinct Sabbath school operations. This institution is the *nursery* of the church. To its members every church is looking for her future enlargement. But if the children are left untaught, in regard to all those truths which are distinctive, what security has she that another will not gather the harvest from the seed which she has herself sown and nurtured? If the truths and principles that are distinctive to any given denomination, are not of enough importance to have them taught to the young —to those by whom the churches of the denomination are to be replenished and perpetuated—then those truths and principles are not of sufficient importance to justify the *existence* of that denomination.[3]

In this context the Sunday school still had an outreach atmosphere. It fulfilled its primary aim for children of believers when at some age of accountability they "joined the church," or "were confirmed," depending on the denomination's understanding of the event. As indicated in the quotation above, there was some pressure for more denominational teaching. But the school still appeared evangelistic, even in churches that opposed the new revivalism with its emphasis on the conversion experience. Either way, the school continued to be identified with children, with those to be brought to membership rather than those already committed. In this light the failure to relate adult classes to the Sunday school becomes more understandable. As the shift toward permanent ties with the church took place, there still was little tendency to broaden the school to train all church members toward greater maturity and service.

As the pioneering stage passed, it was not easy for the Sunday school to find a permanent relationship to the church. With some reason, one study called Sunday schools "ecclesiastical hybrids." [4] On the one hand, contemporary reports described enthusiastically the contribution of Sunday schools to the church and the ministry; two British visitors concluded that they were "the hope of the church." [5] Others criticized them for superseding family training, pastoral instruction, and the church itself. In regard to other church education efforts and to the problem of leadership, the relationship of the Sunday school to the church merits special attention.

Relationship to Other Church Educational Efforts

As the Sunday school arose in the early nineteenth century, it did not move into an utter vacuum. Older and more traditional forms of nurture still were common in most churches, and their supporters hesitated to accept the new agency. Such was the case with catechizing, confirmation training, and preaching, as well as family training in the home.

Catechizing

For a long time in Europe and America catechizing had been a major type of church instruction.[6] As popular summaries of essential doctrines, catechisms had been used for study by children and others since before the Reformation. As to both content and method the practice had advantages. Generally the pastor himself did the catechizing, in public, and often in the setting of worship. Regularly he would preach on the catechism, thus providing background for the summary of belief it included. The parents were expected to "hear" the catechism for their children, with ministerial examination to serve as a spur. Any parent who could read could do that, and with regular attendance upon the preaching he could, to some extent, discuss the meaning of the questions with his children. Matters too difficult for such treatment were handled by the pastor when he himself catechized. Traditional churchmen valued catechetical training in church and home very highly. Bishop Doane wrote that "the Church Catechism is the most wonderful Manual, for the religious nurture of children, that ever has been produced." [7]

However, as church life changed, this customary practice declined. In those churches where it continued as "the regular agency," [8] the Sunday school grew up alongside it. Often there was tension. In many of the newer churches, where no tradition of catechizing existed, the Sunday school substituted for it, frequently providing the only systematic training for the children. Some church leaders even strongly opposed catechisms. Revivalistic groups on the frontier, preferring the simple gospel to dogmatic teaching and lacking trained pastors, wanted lessons they could use and understand—the Bible and moral instruction. Unitarians like William Ellery Channing connected catechisms with the rigid theologies against which they rebelled. Channing wrote a careful criticism of the catechism as a teaching tool, advocating the placing of systematic doctrine last rather than first in Christian teaching and warning that "a catechism is a skeleton, a dead letter, a petrifaction. Wanting life, it can give none." [9] Thus there was misunderstanding, and sometimes conflict, between supporters of traditional catechizing and the newer Sunday schools.

As Sunday schools developed, they adopted some of the practices of the older pattern. The question and answer form of instruction was put to use in teaching the Bible, and early lesson helps for teachers used it. The traditional denominations continued to include catechetical teaching in their Sunday schools. But Sunday school teaching lacked some of the advantages of the older system. The new did not center instruction in the worship of the congregation, or make the pastor the chief teacher and reference person, or include the home as a vital agency. When added to these disadvantages were apprehensions about less and less distinctive doctrinal teaching, as the Bible and practical moral training were emphasized, it is easy to understand how traditional churchmen would hesitate before embracing the Sunday school. In that tension can be seen one aspect of the relationship of the Sunday school to the church in America.

Confirmation Classes

A similar situation existed with regard to confirmation classes. The Lutheran, Episcopal, and Reformed denominations practiced infant baptism and followed the long tradition of confirming the young person at some age of accountability. The revival pattern imposed a type of experience that proved troublesome to assimilate into the framework of that tradition, but those denominations maintained at least some expectation of training for the act of becoming a communicant member. Traditionally the instruction had been given by the pastor and had lasted for several weeks, months, or a year or more. It centered in the customary materials of catechetical training: the Creed, the Lord's Prayer and Sacraments, and the Ten Commandments. In the less traditional, revival-oriented churches the emphasis on the emotional, cataclysmic experience of conversion usually prevented any systematic process of instruction about the meaning of becoming a church member. It was in part against this sacrifice of the developmental and educational process for the sudden emotional conversion, and its consequent doctrinal implications, that Horace Bushnell protested in *Christian Nurture*.

Therefore for many churches the Sunday school, as the only major parish agency of nurture, provided whatever confirmation-like training the new member received. In churches still practicing the older custom, the Sunday school again found itself in competition or uneasy cooperation with an already-established pattern. The authority of the minister and the tie to the sacrament, or quasi-sacramental ceremony of confirmation, in the Protestant churches had given the earlier experience a significance that was hard to recapture without those elements. Thus again the Sunday school found it difficult to relate to an earlier practice. The result was tension in its relationship to the church.

Preaching and Worship Services

From the early days the Sunday school also attached itself to the regular preaching and worship service of the congregation to which it was related. In cities the Sunday school children were usually taken to church as a body, since almost none came from church families or had pews or parents in the sanctuary. Customarily, too, the ensuing school session would review the sermon, although occasionally some teacher would groan over the difficulty of finding any meaning for children in the adult preaching service. When the Sunday school came to include the children of the congregation, it was scheduled before or after the Sunday preaching services. Bishop Doane protested understandably that they had either to hold Sunday school during one of the preaching services or to make for the youngsters a terribly long and arduous day out of Sunday.

Meanwhile, under the impact of revivalism the nature of preaching was shifting.[10] Gradually the function of instructing the congregation in doctrine and practice was giving way to more emphasis on emotional appeals and practical moral instruction. Practices like public catechizing in the setting of congregational worship declined. Earlier the participation of the child and young person in the worship of the congregation had had clear (though not always effective) didactic influences; now those influences were less definite. So again the Sunday school attempted to continue an older strategy, with adaptation that lacked some of the former advantages.[11]

Family Instruction

From its early days the Sunday school was also criticized for superseding family instruction in the faith. In the mid-nineteenth century was there a measurable decline from earlier periods in home religious training? If so, did the Sunday school movement contribute to it?

Certainly there was criticism along this line. Some practices of family training, such as catechetical instruction, seem to have become less common. As the frontier moved westward, family life was often fractured, and as cities developed in the East and the industrial revolution progressed, living patterns changed. But one must doubt whether the average church family one or two hundred years earlier had actually practiced more formal religion in the home. Some writers of the time expressed such doubts.[12]

At any rate, leaders of the Sunday school objected strongly to the charge that it was superseding the family. They claimed that it could not and did not try to be a substitute for parental teaching. Rather, it performed the duty of the Christian parent for children doomed to "the evils of spiritual orphanage." [13] In fact, the Sunday school saw itself as a definite help to family religious training. Lyman Beecher's decision to enroll his own children in its classes recognized that it could give valuable supplementary teaching even to children of the manse. By 1858 the ASSU report claimed that "it was never intended that the Sunday schools should interfere with the domestic instruction so clearly required in the scriptures." The report continued, stating a very common viewpoint:

The family is a divine institution, and no earthly power can ever excuse parents from the duties which it involves in reference to the religious training of the young. . . . and numerous facts show, most conclusively, that family religion has been greatly promoted by the divine blessing upon Sabbath-schools.

Pious parents are greatly *assisted* in the religious training of their children by the labours of the godly Sunday school-teacher. The lessons of the Sunday-school are carried to *the home,* and furnish occasion for the study of the Bible and matter for religious inquiry and conversation; and hence it is found that no persons are more in love with this blessed institution than are those parents who are most diligent in the exercises of family religion. Where one parent has attempted to shift his responsibilities upon the Sunday-school teacher, it is safe to assume that a thousand have been quickened and encouraged in the good work of family instruction, and that ten thousand children, by the blessing of God, have received religious impressions in the Sabbath-school which will result in making many Christian *homes* when these little ones shall come to years of maturity.[14]

Beyond that, the report said, the Sunday school overcame the failures of the million parents not connected with the church who were indisposed or incompetent to give their children Christian training.

Occasionally someone would outline the complementary functions of school and home. For instance, one wrote that parents should give their children "incidental religious instruction, as it might be called for or rendered appropriate by their circumstances or their conduct, while the Sunday school teacher is giving systematic instruction upon the facts and truths, the principles and doctrines, of the Gospel." [15]

The manuals urged Sunday school teachers to call on the homes of their children, to give pastoral-type aid to their families, and to invite non-churchgoers to attend. The description of the Northampton schools by Reed and Matheson pictures how the ideal school would work, if it followed such suggestions.[16]

So Sunday school and home did not overlap as did school and pastoral instruction; cooperation came more naturally. Pious parents, and presumably impious ones as well, wanted the church to give their children religious training. Many of them felt inadequate to teach their children. Although many commentators pointed out the dangers of letting the Sunday school take over what the family should do, the school moved right in as either supplement to or substitute for family training.

Adult Study Groups

Another type of church instruction related to the Sunday school was adult study. Many pastors, like Justin Edwards of the church near Andover Theological Seminary, taught Bible classes in their own congregations.[17] During the 1820's, as lecturer in the seminary, Edwards advocated merging the Sunday school and Bible classes into one movement. By 1829 an "American Bible Class Society" issued its *Second Annual Report,* which stated:

> Bible classes greatly increase the efficiency of all other benevolent institutions. They apply to the multitude the stupendous truths circulated by the Bible society; they prepare teachers for the sabbath schools; they supply materials for education societies to work up; they furnish men for the service of missionary societies, foreign and domestic; and by increasing the number of faithful ministers and pious parents and holy men in the different departments of business, they will multiply beyond calculation the members and the means of every charitable society upon earth.[18]

The society claimed a history of seventeen years, five or six hundred classes from nine denominations, and sixty to eighty thousand members. Frederick W. Packard of the ASSU concluded that "Bible Classes are an essential appendage to the Sunday-school" for two reasons: they teach those too old for the ordinary exercises, and they help supply teacher vacancies.[19]

Such classes probably furnished the earliest regular training of Sunday school teachers, and leaders often urged them for that purpose. Emphasizing the broader purpose, however, Archibald Alexander in 1829 suggested enlarging the system by joining "infant schools, Sunday-schools, Bible classes, and adult schools, as all parts of one system . . . so that the church would then become what it was designed to be—a great school for disciples of all ages." [20]

Despite such efforts, however, adult Sunday school programs before the Civil War neither prospered nor became an integral part of the Sunday school. The failures of this effort underscored some of the weaknesses becoming apparent in the growing movement: its identification with children, its lack of integration into full church life, its inadequate amateur teaching, and the casual spare-time image fostered by these characteristics.

Youth Groups

There were also some special attempts to teach young people from the years of late childhood to early adulthood. Often persons in this age group became regular teachers in the school, causing problems because of their immaturity.[21] Others, probably most, tended to drift away as they undertook new adult responsibilities but were not yet ready for church leadership (which the church was often not ready to expect of them anyway, except in certain ways, such as Sunday school teaching). Out of concern for this "lost" group arose a variety of educational and other programs for young people.

By 1860 these efforts were not institutionalized in efficient national patterns, but the seeds were there for later growth. The Young Men's Christian Association, begun in London in 1844, had its first chapter in the United States in Boston in 1851, and by 1860 counted some 205 local organizations with some twenty-five thousand members.[22] Some local church youth groups met on Sunday for study and fellowship, and some ministers gathered young people into continuing classes for Bible study and even elementary theological education. Public high schools were not general until after the Civil War, and the academies and colleges educated only a small propor- tion of persons of that age. Structurally, therefore, these per- sons were adults, suffering the same lack of school opportunity as other non-children. The emphasis upon conversion and the identifying of the Sunday school with children, in an environ- ment when schooling ended at late childhood for most people, resulted in a feeling of "getting out of school," which undoubt- edly made it difficult to hold this age group in regular study. But the need was growing, as young people became more dis- tinctively a group. In the face of the challenge, the Sunday school and the church were both slow to respond. The prevail- ing tensions of their interrelationship added to the problem.

Parochial Schools

By the 1850's there was another strategy alternative—the parochial or church-controlled day school. By 1860 the Ro- man Catholics were committing themselves to that option. For them the problem had been increasingly acute, as the common schools tended to be Protestant. In the 1840's in New York

City Bishop Hughes had fought for tax funds for Catholic schools, and had lost. By 1852 a council exhorted bishops whenever possible to establish parochial schools in their dioceses.[23] By 1884 the Third Plenary Council in Baltimore commanded "a truly Christian and Catholic education . . . [in] parochial schools" unless special exception was granted.[24] Feeling besieged and isolated, with an immigrant population, yet with high ethnic intensity and tight ecclesiastical organization, the Catholic church could sustain a private religious school system. The story of that effort constitutes one of the truly heroic chapters in the history of American education, for during a half century a predominantly poor minority group bucked the successful growth of the American common schools and established at considerable sacrifice a system that seemed better designed for Rome and Europe than the United States.[25]

For the purposes of the study of Protestant educational strategy, the Catholic development supports the analysis made here. For one thing, the same options the Protestants chose were not only live alternatives for the Catholics, but they were utilized by them before, during, and after the decision for parochial schools. Wherever Catholic children attended public schools, the parish often established Sunday schools (or their equivalents) much like those of the Protestant churches. Older forms of church instruction were continued even where parochial schools arose, especially catechetical training in connection with major church and/or sacramental occasions in the child's life. Interestingly, too, Catholic concentration upon children in parochial and other forms of schooling left that church as poorly furnished as the Protestant for serious education of the older youth and adult members of the church.

Just as the Catholic commitment to parochial schools was not inevitable or unanimous, neither was the Protestant rejection of that option. The most dramatic Protestant experiment in parochial schools was made by the Presbyterian church in the 1840's and 1850's. Lewis J. Sherrill's study of that movement traces the factors involved.[26] Increasingly upset over the growing secularism in the common schools, the Old School Presbyterian General Assembly in 1846 and 1847 adopted a plan of parochial schools. Powerful ecclesiastical forces debated for over a decade, with the Princeton Seminary faculty leading the fight for the plan. According to Sherrill's count, some 264 Presbyterian schools were actually established.

But the effort failed. Sherrill concluded that the overwhelming reason was that "an entire educational system [was] not necessary to perpetuate the Presbyterian church." [27] His statement gives further evidence of the Protestant consensus:

> As if by a sure instinct, the church as a whole detected that the necessity for general education in Calvinism's past had been an accident, due merely to popular ignorance and state indifference. Presbyterians throughout America recognized a vast difference between those and American conditions. And accordingly, the church was not convinced that Presbyterian parochial schools held the solution to the problem of keeping religion in education. . . . That is, the duty to give education is a responsibility resting on society as a whole for the benefit of society as a whole; and not upon only a part of society for the benefit merely of that part. . . . The very facts here brought out are significant evidence of the community of interest and belief of the Presbyterian church with the Christian portion of American society. . . . The community is greater than the divergence; so much greater that the Presbyterian church quietly refused to be maneuvered to a position of isolation.

The differences are not great enough to justify an entire educational system erected for the purpose of preserving them. That portion of the parochial curriculum of religious education which would distinguish it from the religious education of another evangelical denomination turned out to be so small that only a relatively simple system is necessary to provide it.[28]

Most of the Protestant denominations agreed. Those newly emerging as significant groups in America had little distinctive tradition to defend and were quite willing for the combination of public school and Sunday school to carry the weight of the teaching they thought essential. Other mainline traditional denominations, such as Episcopalian, Dutch Reformed, and Lutheran, were more tempted by the parochial school option, but by and large they too settled for the "relatively simple system." Only the Roman Catholics and a few other churches with ethnic isolation (often symbolized by a foreign language), traditional worship patterns, and an ecclesiastical hierarchy that could mobilize members for a concerted effort chose the parochial school alternative. By 1860, therefore, the overwhelming mass of American Protestant church members and their denominations had rejected parochial, church-controlled education. The result was a serious if somewhat ambivalent commitment to the Sunday school as religious partner to the common school.

Denominational Colleges and Seminaries

Alongside these efforts came the astonishing rise of denominational colleges and theological seminaries during the pre-Civil War period. By far the great majority of colleges before 1860 were established by denominations, motivated in part by sectarian jealousies and competition.[29] The most important reason usually given was the need for trained ministers in the church. Anti-Catholic sentiment played a part, but may have been more useful in getting money from wealthy donors in eastern cities than in giving direction to the actual establishment of colleges. In the long perspective, Protestant-Catholic rivalry can be interpreted as sectarian rivalry.

But why should denominations establish their own colleges when they felt little need for church day schools at the lower levels? That question provokes another: with primary education increasingly "common," despite efforts to make the Sunday school sectarian, how could a denomination maintain its distinctiveness? The answer lay in its leadership, especially the clergy. Their training in college and seminary taught them to distinguish between their particular doctrines and practices and the common Christianity their laymen shared with others in benevolent societies. In 1837 Charles Hodge articulated that viewpoint:

> Wherever the field of operation is common to different denominations, and the proper means for its cultivation are also the same for all, there is an obvious reason why all should unite. These conditions meet with regard to the Bible and Tract Societies, and in many important respects in regard to Sunday School Unions. There are other cases in which voluntary societies of a denominational character may be either indispensable or highly desirable. On the other hand there are cases for which ecclesiastical organizations appear to us to be entitled to decided preference. To this class belong the work of educating ministers of the gospel, and that of missions.[30]

However, as Hodge suggested, in supporting both Sunday schools and colleges American Protestantism was building its educational effort upon two different strategies. On the one hand, spurred by the Reformation, the church was developing a parish system of universal education for every Christian. Through the dual pattern of common school and Sunday school, Protestantism hoped to convert persons to Christ and his church and to help them learn how to live accordingly. On the other hand, with medieval precedent, the church sought to provide educated leadership to serve the distinctive denominational traditions. For that purpose it established institutions of higher learning outside the local parish. And, unfortunately, the two parts were seldom seen in relationship to each other. Histories of the one usually ignore the other, and contemporary documents show the same separation.

As apprenticeship training for the ministry was succeeded by schools to train ministers, the denominations established many small, isolated seminaries. Their candidates studied theology in the tradition of the denomination. They often lacked training in how to oversee the Sunday school for the people in the parish. The minister's concern for protecting the tradition or his eagerness to evangelize through his pulpit ministry made it hard for him to relate easily to the Sunday school.[31] The next section, which discusses the problem of leadership, pursues this question further, but the existence of separate and different kinds of educational institutions for church leaders and for church members contributed to tension between the Sunday school and the church as defined denominationally.

Thus the Sunday school developed into a major agency of Protestant church education, inevitably related to other forms of church education such as catechetical and confirmation classes, the sermon, family training, adult Bible classes, youth groups, parochial schools, and denominational colleges and seminaries. The list betrays a lack of clear Protestant church educational strategy during this period. The Protestants failed to devise a pattern to unite the various agencies into one comprehensive system. In committing themselves to such a wide variety of educational efforts and institutions, the churches committed themselves to considerable frustration.

The very real gains of the Sunday school movement, then, must be seen in the light of these uncoordinated and often conflicting developments. In its great heyday in the nineteenth century, American Protestantism bore within its fundamental strategy of church education inconsistencies and weaknesses that were to contribute to serious problems in the twentieth century.

The Problem of Leadership

By the time Sunday schools began in America, their models in Britain had shifted from paid to volunteer teachers. In the new land the volunteer lay teacher soon became a symbol of the Sunday school movement. Various advantages were claimed: volunteers enabled the school to be maintained inexpensively; the example of dedicated Christian laymen and women contributing time and effort in itself proved valuable to the young scholars; and occasionally a writer would praise especially the use of young people and young adults for their influence over the children. Also, more teachers could be used, giving each fewer pupils and thus compensating for the smaller amount of time spent in Sunday school. The further claim was made that the system put "not theologians or polemics, but plain men and women of right Christian experience" [32] at the head of Sunday school classes. In his sermon to the ASSU in 1839 Samuel S. Schmucker, Lutheran theological professor conspicuous in general Protestant affairs, congratulated the movement for employing "the lay agency":

> Before the era of Sunday-schools, the duty of religious instruction was supposed to appertain only to ministers, and in some countries, also to the village school master. But since the happy conception of the immortal Raikes, the whole body of Christians may be literally "priests under God," the number of instructors can be multiplied to any desirable extent, and the purifying, elevating, saving knowledge of the truth of God be carried to every inmate of every hovel in the land. [33]

Thus spokesmen for the Sunday school claimed significant values from the practice of using volunteer lay leadership.

More common, however, were voices criticizing the quality of teaching in the schools. Many churchmen worried about the number of "non-professors" of religion who were teachers. In those days of revivals churches included many persons who, because they had not experienced a conversion that fitted the standard pattern, were not "professed" Christians. Sunday school reports expressed constant concern that such teachers have a conversion, and one can imagine the pressures put upon them in revival sessions. The 1842 *Annual Report* estimated that more than a hundred thousand persons had been brought into the kingdom chiefly through the Sunday school, and that probably twenty-five to thirty thousand of them "received the truth into their hearts while engaged in the benevolent labour of teaching it to others." [34]

The *Annual Report* of 1841 expressed another common complaint—the youth of the teachers:

It is a matter of deep regret to your board, that so inconsiderable a proportion of teachers in our Sunday-schools, are persons of immature years and experience. It is believed that many who would prefer to attend school as pupils, are constrained by necessity to occupy the place of teachers, notwithstanding their consciousness of incompetency, because their seniors neglect or decline to serve.

It cannot be expected that youth, themselves just out of the hands of tutors and governors, should generally command that degree of respect, confidence, and obedience, which is quite indispensable to the order and improvement of a class. And, especially in the schools of this country, where "liberty and equality" is (we might almost say) a cradle motto, the restraint of moral influence in some form, seems the only substitute for naked authority or power. It is a matter of unfeigned regret to those who are accustomed to visit schools in various parts of the country, that so little respect is manifested for the office of a teacher, particularly in schools and classes of boys; and that so much of levity, insubordination, and irregularity is allowed. We would earnestly commend this evil and its remedy to the consideration of our fellow-labourers and friends. It is not improbable, that children who attend our schools from well ordered families, may suffer irreparable injury from the examples of disobedience and contempt of authority which they witness, unless they are promptly checked.[35]

One writer advocated a larger class under one good teacher rather than smaller groups under inexperienced ones.[36]

More common still were complaints that teaching, in general, was poor. Even a zealous missionary like B. W. Chidlaw confessed in his autobiography that "the great draw-back in our missionary work in those early times was the want of qualified officers and teachers, men and women of faith, of Bible knowledge, apt to teach, and blessed with continuance in well doing." [37] The early Sunday school records provide frequent implications that class sessions lacked much regarding order and sound learning. The following, "Rules for Sunday Schools," printed on cards in 1824, and to be learned in a discussion of discipline, suggests the level of classroom learning processes:

1. I must always mind the Superintendent and all the Teachers of this School.
2. I must come every Sunday, and be here when School goes in.
3. I must go to my seat as soon as I come in.
4. I MUST ALWAYS BE STILL.
5. I must not leave my seat till School goes out.
6. I must take good care of my book.
7. I must not *lean* on the next boy.
8. I must walk softly in the School.
9. I must not make a noise by the Church door or School door, but must go in as soon as I come there.
10. I must always go to Church.
11. I must behave well in the street when I am going to Church.
12. I must walk softly into Church.

13. I must sit still in my place till Church goes out.
14. I must go away from the Church as soon as I go out.
15. I, A. B., *must always mind the Superintendents and all the Teachers of this school.*[38]

Furthermore, there was a connection between the type of lesson materials used and the quality of teaching. The early lessons were generally learned by memory, so that all the young teachers had to do was "hear" the catechism or Bible verses indiscriminately selected by the pupils.[39] As "Selected Lessons" from the Bible came into common use, and then Bible Questions, more was expected of the teacher. The concerns then expanded beyond disciplinary problems to the matter of what was being learned. Committed by strategy to largely untrained lay teachers and by practice to young, often immature ones, the Sunday school faced a serious handicap whenever it tried to improve lesson materials. At each stage the new materials had to be taught by those who had grown up under the older, less satisfactory system and who therefore tended to teach what and how they had been taught. By the 1840's public school systems were developing normal schools to help prepare more effective teachers. Sunday school leaders from that time on became convinced that an equally serious program to train Sunday school teachers was essential to the movement. But the commitment to volunteer leadership hampered development of any serious teacher training, and no adequate answer was found before 1860.

The problem related also to the minister's function. Old-line denominations with learned clergymen expected the minister to teach. He was the congregation's catechist, teaching elder, and instructor in matters of faith. How were these new lay teachers to relate to him and his traditional role as teacher?

In many places the minister became the teacher of the teachers. A surprising number of ministerial and Sunday school references speak of weekly meetings of the minister with his teachers. Clergymen would give what Stephen H. Tyng, strong Episcopalian supporter of the ASSU, called a "familiar personal lecture" to edify and prepare them for teaching the next Sunday.[40] Alonzo Potter, former college professor, gave weekday lectures to his teachers on the school lessons, and was proud that they "prepared themselves for their teaching with almost as great diligence as he. . . ." [41] The Rev. Asa Bullard strongly approved such practices:

> By attending the teachers' meeting, the pastor increases the power of his ministry. The teachers become the instruments with which he works. Teachers, it has been well said, are the pastor's colleagues to the extent of their ability. He electrotypes himself, as it were, upon them, and through them becomes himself a teacher in every class in the school. His remarks and illustrations of truths will be repeated by them in every class. He becomes himself acquainted with the lessons, so that his prayers for the school, and his own teachings from the pulpit, his remarks at the school and the concerts, and his personal addresses to the members of his school, as he meets them in their homes or by the way, will be more appropriate and practical.[42]

Professor Archibald Alexander's appeal to the alumni of Princeton Seminary in 1834 shows the possibility of fruitful cooperation:

> By means of Sunday schools, now so widely extended over the church, the faithful pastor is furnished with a troop of auxiliaries, in the faithful discharge of his duty, unknown to our fathers, and which should be appreciated as one of the distinguished blessings which God has granted to his church in our days. . . .[43]

But the weight of evidence suggests that there was more tension between the old and new educational leadership than such words would imply. These excerpts from Bishop Doane illustrate how strong the feeling of tension could be:

In their original use, Sunday Schools were well conceived. They met a present necessity. But they have grown into a habit of the Church; much to the hindrance of its purity and unity. . . . They have superseded Pastoral Instruction. . . . They have introduced a body of teachers, without responsibility; and, often, more zealous, than instructed or discreet. They have become an organization, outside of the Church, and independent of it. They are like the Vigilance Committee in California; in the place of law and order, of office and authority. This is where they are not closely and constantly under the direction of the pastor. Where they are, they do but add to his labours, and lay another burden on his overloaded Sunday: not to speak of the difficulties, and disorders, and dissensions, and divisions, to which they constantly tend, and which they often introduce. . . . If there is a Sunday School in the parish, the pastor must be in it, and of it, and through it, and over it. And it will cost him more time, more toil, more care, than the proper system of the Church: and with small satisfaction; and no certainty, in its results.[44]

Quite frequent were appeals to the clergy to take more responsibility in the affairs of the schools attached to their churches. Through the years the tone of such appeals in the ASSU publications varied from optimism to pessimism, from exhortation to complaints.

One factor contributing to the tension was that the ASSU did not include ministers on its Board of Managers. The real leadership was thus kept out of clerical hands. The lay directorate, after easing the clergy out of the highest responsibility, employed them as "expert staff" in such functions as publication committee members, agents, missionaries, and supporters. The problem of the relationship of the benevolent societies to the church was manifest in the tenuous and ambivalent part played by the traditional ecclesiastical leaders, the clergy, in the affairs of the societies. The trend away from "union" agencies toward denominational organizations was in part an attempt to re-establish ecclesiastical, i.e., clerical, control over the new institutions.[45]

While at the top of the organized Sunday school movement the laymen were in control, at the local parish level the situation was not quite so simple. There the superintendent often subtly challenged the minister, and sometimes won. But the Sunday schools sooner or later had to relate for security and support to a church, and when they did the pastors became more powerful. As the ministers were striving to develop responsible stewardship toward the new denominational agencies of education and publication, agents of the ASSU were having trouble getting into local congregations to make their appeals. However, in the many congregations that either had no resident minister or had a pastor unable or unwilling to teach the teachers, the local lay leaders became accustomed to operating independently and on their own resources. Thus a combination of forces worked to keep the Sunday school leadership somewhat separated from the traditional church leaders.

Another factor was the training and work of the ministers. Increasingly most ministerial candidates grew up through the Sunday school as it had come to include more and more of the children of the church. One favorite "field work" experience for seminary students during this period was Sunday school work, either as missionaries or agents, or as local school superintendents or teachers. At Yale, Andover, Princeton, Auburn, and other seminaries, all centers of support for the benevolent societies, students were quite active in Sunday school work and went out in large numbers to become positive supporters of the movement. Presbyterian and Congregational missionary strategy called for settled, trained pastors so that their continuing relationship with and control over the Sunday schools of their churches was important. The more itinerant ministerial strategies of the West would not impose such ministerial influence upon the schools, nor would untrained ministers be able to provide as much intellectual guidance of the teachers. Gradually ministers in local congregations became more involved in the Sunday schools as their denominations moved into the field with their own education and publication societies.

One further factor was the use of women in the Sunday school. From Robert Raikes' first afternoon session, the Sunday school used women teachers. Here was a radical "democratizing" of church leadership, for women remained the large majority among Sunday school teachers. Converted and eager to serve, women often were the natural choices to teach children. After all, was not the Sunday school an extension of the home, and had not mothers often done much of the religious teaching there? The women, not allowed to assume official church responsibilities, turned to the Sunday school and other benevolent societies as significant channels for their religious zeal. As teachers in the Sunday school, they became indispensable to the new movement.

With church leadership still a masculine preserve, however, any movement identified with feminine activity and leadership could not easily be assimilated into the ecclesiastical structure. No doubt individual ministers rejoiced over the diligent work of their women members in the Sunday school. But the hybrid ecclesiastical nature of the movement was furthered by the fact of predominant female influence in the actual working of the school. As difficult as it was to resolve the problems involved in relating lay leadership to the long tradition of theologically-educated clerical instruction in the church, the situation was even more complex when much of the lay leadership was constitutionally unable to share official ecclestical responsibility with the minister. Perhaps, too, the predominance of women in the movement intensified its identification with children, making more difficult the working out of forms of higher education in the Sunday school, for advanced education had been less home- and woman-centered than schooling for children.

Thus the matter of leadership demonstrated and contributed to the problem of relating the Sunday school to the church. As part of the amazing rise of vigorous lay Christian activity in nineteenth-century America, the Sunday school could proudly boast of its place in that significant development. But as a religious institution the Sunday school had to be connected firmly with the church in its emerging denominational forms. At national and local levels the prevailing relationships created tension between old and new patterns of leadership.

Implications

During these decades, therefore, the Sunday school was an agency adjunct to the church as well as to the public school. Ultimately it was to become an agency of church education, because of its religious nature. But the implications of that ambivalent relationship during this formative period help show the place of the Sunday school in the educational, ecclesiastical, and cultural-social history of the United States.

First, the relationship of the Sunday school to the church proved difficult because it originated outside the organized church. First in England, and then in America, this was so. In his history of the ASSU Rice reminded the church of that background:

> Hence the Sunday-schools were of necessity maintained in partial or total independence of church control, although often held in the churches. Even a generation or so later, when the church "came to itself," it did not apparently realize its mistake, except to discover that these schools in the church should prop-

erly be conducted and controlled by the church. It sharply censured Sunday-school workers for not at first heartily assenting to such control. The church leaders forgot, or were entirely ignorant of, the fact that their predecessors in the early history of the Sunday-school movement had not welcomed the schools, and had thus kept them outside for more than a generation. The schools had so long been in the habit of managing their own affairs, and of providing for their own support, enforced by this sentiment of the church, that it required an educational campaign of long continuance to undo and correct this habit and, smoothly and satisfactorily, to bring even church Sunday-schools into organic harmony with the church. And the school was long left to pay its own expense after it came under church control. . . .[46]

In one sense the long story of the American Sunday school could be interpreted as the progressive baptism of the Sunday school into ecclesiastical respectability. The process was rarely smooth, and the result never fully achieved.

Second, from the Sunday school's involvement in the benevolent society movement of the nineteenth century came tensions in relating to the organized church. After an initial period of doubt, in the confusion following the Revolution and disestablishment, most church leaders supported the movements of organized benevolence.[47] Now denied the coercion of legal establishment, church and philanthropic leaders embraced the voluntary societies as an excellent way of harnessing the committed zeal of dedicated Christians and turning it into a mighty wave of moral force throughout the new nation. Although their motives have been attacked by several students of the "Protestant Crusade," [48] these were men with memories of social order and control that went back deep into the Middle Ages. For them the new situation called merely for a change in tactics from coercion to moral suasion —they never doubted that the goal of an ordered society according to God's will and for man's good was one whit different under republican government than it had been under other types in previous ages. Their crusade was to move men to responsible citizenship through moral enlightenment; hence their campaigns were essentially to instruct society about right and wrong, and their revival techniques were systematically-employed means to persuade men's emotions toward the right response. The Sunday school belonged to that movement.

It was inevitable, given the long tradition of priestly power in society, that critics would attack such efforts. Early opposition came from those who had most feared the previous establishment: the leaders of small sects who saw new threats to their religious liberty from the insidious but powerful suasion pressure. Called the "anti-mission movement," these spokesmen protested against these "inventions of man, the product of scheming doctors of divinity whose money-gathering propensities and zeal for organization threatened the future of the faith." [49]

Despite these critics and the forces of denominationalism which were much more powerful later, the "crusade" mounted its great effort. Foster summarizes:

> The Evangelical movement which restored the prestige of religion and gave the United States its Protestant character was not, at this stage [c. 1828], a denominational effort. The financing of education for the ministry, the organization and administration of missionary effort both foreign and domestic, the promotion of the Evangelical youth movement in its various aspects, and the production and distribution of propaganda in its numerous forms, as well as the general direction of lay activity and, to a degree, the formulation of doctrine, were all the work of societies requiring no test for membership other than a small fee. Societies were a central fact of the country's religious life during its most formative years.[50]

The historical situation gave impetus to common efforts of this sort. Most of the American church traditions had come from lands where there was only one established church, and many had known that reality in the colonies. In the early 1800's the need for political unity tended to make other union efforts popular. The separate expressions of religious pluralism had their histories, too, but they had to fight against the forces toward union. Thus, basic in the Sunday school movement was the "union principle," the hope that through emphasis on the Bible and common Christianity the Sunday school could bring into effective joint schooling all Christians whose church affiliations tended to divided them from one another. The ASSU affirmed this in its 1833 *Annual Report:*

> It should be distinctly known throughout the land that the first grand principle of our association is UNION—that as a society we recognize the existence of various evangelical denominations only so far as to avoid their points of difference—that there is no representation of them, as such, in our body, nor of us, in theirs. We rest on the broad basis of the Christian church; and esteeming every true disciple of the Lord Jesus Christ as one with us in this general purpose we invite his co-operation in building up the kingdom of our common Redeemer, on the foundation of the apostles and prophets—Jesus Christ himself being the chief cornerstone.[51]

Its historian, aware of the importance of the relationship to the church, clarified by suggesting that technically the ASSU was neither undenominational, antidenominational, nor interdenominational, but was rather "a voluntary union of individual Christians, of different religious views and creeds, cooperating for the purpose of promoting religious education through Bible study and the establishment of Sunday-schools." [52] The Sunday school therefore represented the evangelical movement in America, a movement which in ways threatened the denominations as they developed their own structures. Thus the Sunday school movement, broader in membership and less exacting in its membership qualifications than any denomination, yet quite similar to the denominations in its fundamental voluntary nature and purpose, became a more extreme expression of the voluntary principle characterizing American Christianity.

In this way the ASSU served almost as another denomination, with its own constituency, its own missionary goals and projects, its own benevolence system, administrative structure, and theological reference system. As an institutional expression for the pan-denominational movement, it afforded its followers the opportunity for service and a continuing center for loyalty alongside similar provisions by the denominations. And, although its influence waned before the Civil War, it was to revive later in the nineteenth century.[53]

At the local level, too, the Sunday school existed as an institution alongside the church. It was lodged in the basement of the sanctuary or in an educational building, symbolically separate from or perhaps subordinate to—or even dominating —the "church" building proper. Persons could belong officially to both the Sunday school and the local church. It was easy for the former to reflect the free church tradition as the revival movement was shaping it, and for the latter to have traditional and formal liturgy. In the community the Sunday school leaders and members crossed denominational lines. The Sunday school's lay atmosphere was pan-Protestant. The local church tended to be more strongly clerical, and more separatist in its community effect. By 1860 the two existed as parallel institutions. The denominational forms of church experience had begun to take control, and the long gradual process of assimilating the Sunday school into the organizational framework of the church was under way. But the differences in origin and practice on the local level, intensified by similarities and overlapping of personnel and program, created problems for Protestantism in the task of developing a consistent and effective educational strategy.

The union principle bore fruit in several ways. With its broad base of lay involvement and control, it contributed to the feeling of national unity. As noted earlier, the Sunday school movement was quite patriotic. As the tensions leading to the Civil War accumulated, the ASSU warned its agents to avoid conflicts over the slavery issue. In 1857 one speaker called it "a Union-saving Institution," proclaiming that "South Carolina and Massachusetts quarrel in politics, but the American Sunday School Union constrains them to exchange the kiss of peace and to work shoulder to shoulder in this great cause of Christian love.[54] During the war some of its missionaries were welcomed on both sides of the battle lines, and afterwards its great convention movements brought together again Protestant representatives from all sections. No doubt the professions exceeded the practice in many cases, but with its lay character and simple theological commitment the movement did seem to weather the crisis better than most of the denominations and many of the other benevolent societies.[55]

Probably more important was the contribution of the Sunday school to the "common faith" of nineteenth-century lay Protestantism. Emphasizing the Bible and morality, the Sunday school used an Evangelical "creed" which ruled out Unitarians and made theological liberals uncomfortable. This "creed" was described from time to time, as in this typical list of a "few elementary truths" to be taught to little children:

1. God made me.
2. Christ died for me.
3. My soul will live forever.
4. If I repent and believe in Christ, I shall be forever happy.
5. If I die in sin, I shall be forever miserable.
6. I must obey my parents, and those that have rule over me.

7. I must keep holy the Sabbath Day.
8. I must read the Scriptures, and learn from them what I am to believe and do.[56]

Or, at the adult level:

> In the doctrines of the supremacy of the inspired scriptures, as the rule of faith and duty—the lost state of man by nature, and his exposure to endless punishment in a future world—his recovery only by the influence of the Holy Spirit—the necessity of faith, repentance and holy living, with an open confession of the saviour before men, and the duty of complying with his ordinances of baptism and the Lord's Supper—in these doctrines we find the essential and leading truths of the Christian system; in the reception of these doctrines we agree, and with God's help, we endeavor to teach and inculcate them on all whom we can properly reach.[57]

This "Sunday school faith" became quite common among the laity. They saw it as stressing what was necessary to be saved; and were not beliefs necessary to salvation the most important things to be taught? Like the kindred theology of the revival movement, as preached by a man like Charles G. Finney, the "Sunday school faith" resembled "orthodox Calvinism." It was basic to the teaching of many denominations and supplementary for others. For still others, like the Unitarians, it was highly sectarian and therefore suspect. The Sunday school served as an instrument for establishing and perpetuating that faith.

However, like the institution of the Sunday school, this common system of belief found itself suspended between two powerful movements, each based in a more massive institution. On the one side, leaders of the church found the theology too broad, too weak, too indistinct to serve the more particular needs of organized denominations. Theologically-sensitive clergymen criticized the reduction of distinctive denominational traditions to a lowest common denominator. Although the predominant atmosphere was Protestant, translating that atmosphere into specific lessons and programs proved difficult.

On the other side, the public school was trying to teach a common Christianity. It too represented a broad Protestant atmosphere, one too broad to be limited to the major Evangelical tradition, as some of Horace Mann's antagonists defined it. As Packard and Mann demonstrated in their debates, this Sunday school theology would not fit the common school package, at least not in Massachusetts in the 1840's. The Sunday school did not have enough religion for the church; it had too much for the public schools.

Even though by 1860 there was little discernible difference between the religious influences of Sunday school and public school—the inability of the Presbyterian parochial schools to distinguish themselves enough from public schools had hurt their cause—the fact of having religious school on the religious day of the week, completely separate from the common schools on weekdays, was significant. James Hastings Nichols rightly summarizes the effect:

> The leading educators of this first generation of the public schools were all agreed that the teaching of morality was the paramount responsibility of the public schools. But this was a morality of natural law, the ethical principles generally acknowledged in the common life, even apart from the church and revelation, although in no way incompatible with the teachings of the latter. The meaning of this typical parallelism of public school and Sunday School is, I think, that Protestants have accepted the compartmentalization of faith and culture.[58]

To the children taught in this parallel system of schools the affairs of life would tend to belong to the common school, those of religion separate from real life in the Sunday school. Sidney Mead states that

> Most important was the implication that only what the religious "sects" held and taught in common (the rationalists' "essentials

of every religion") was relevant to the public welfare of the new commonwealth. For the obverse side of this was that what each group held peculiar to itself, and hence what gave it its only reason for separate existence, was irrelevant to the general welfare for the whole commonwealth. No wonder that a sense of irrelevance has always haunted the most sectarian religious leaders in America.[59]

The effect was to make Protestant Christianity as thus defined irrelevant, and since it was the predominant religion in the society, to make religion itself irrelevant.

Furthermore, excluding this particular form of religion from the common schools cleared the way for another form of religious belief, a broader secular American humanism, to emerge. The questions the "sectarians" posed to Horace Mann would have to be faced ultimately not only by their sectarian successors in the denominations but also by Mann's Christian successors in the public schools and society at large. When by definition what was common became the accepted belief, then through the years a lowest-common-denominator reductionism became probable.

Thus its identification with broad Protestant Christianity seriously affected the Sunday school as an institution parallel to the public schools. Similarly, this identification affected its relationship with the church, increasingly defined by its denominational structures. Like the ASSU, the denominations in America were voluntary organizations formed for a purpose. But the denominations, controlled by traditional structures and influenced strongly by clergymen, wanted the Sunday school to teach their denominational beliefs and traditions as well as the broader evangelical "creed." No "common Christianity" could satisfy all in a time of rising denominationalism. Church leaders who wanted Sunday schools under ecclesiastical control soon formed denominational Sunday school organizations and publication societies, beginning in 1825. They could not risk allowing a religious educational agency to be controlled by a union society that did not teach their denominational beliefs. They were unwilling to accept the "church" implications of the Sunday school: its lay ministry, its own evangelistic and missionary projects, its own buildings, its forms of worship and study, its own centralized apparatus, and its own set of beliefs.

Thus by the 1830's the movement was becoming more denominational. The so-called "Babel period" in Sunday school curriculum history must be interpreted as evidence of the attempt to control the schools of the churches and to find the materials and program to nurture that denominational expression.

What was involved was the definition of the Sunday school: was it primarily an instrument of missionary evangelism for evangelical Protestantism as a whole, or was it primarily an instrument of nurture for the various denominations with their distinctive beliefs and practices? Although in its early years the former was the Sunday school's primary definition, by 1860 the school was headed toward the latter. But the reality of the earlier direction lay deep within it, so that the tension between the two could not be settled merely by shifting organizational control.

But that question really was part of a still larger one: What was the church in this new society? Was it an American moral and spiritual voluntary agency, a new kind of "lay church" which, by instructing people in its common Christian principles, would ensure an effective republican society? Or was it a pluralism of different denominations, each holding to its distinctive heritage and therefore needing to control the nurturing agencies by which successive generations were instructed in the faith? Caught in the tension between these alternatives, the Sunday school movement exemplifies the search by the American church for an understanding of its own nature in the new setting. In the discernible trend from union to denominational organization can be seen another witness to the development of that distinctive American pattern of church life, the denomination.

Despite the inclusion of Sunday schools in the church, however, the relationships were not always clear or pleasant. The churches felt ambivalent about adopting the new instrument, for it meant giving up at least the appearance of some older forms and the embracing of something new, the origins of which were not above question.

But by 1860 the enduring pattern had emerged: the union Sunday school movement had given way in large measure to denominational education organizations. Evidence supports the conclusion of Smith, Handy, and Loetscher that "in the second quarter of the nineteenth century, spokesmen for all of the more churchly Protestant traditions—Lutheran, Reformed and Presbyterian, Anglican—arose to challenge the nondenominational unity which was forming"; these spokesmen advocated having the church "conduct its own educational and missionary enterprises." [60] In the early years there was some hostility by the union forces to denominational Sunday schools, but gradually as the ecclesiastical groups became powerful the union movement cooperated with them.

Had the union Sunday school movement had its way, along with other advocates of a common Christianity, American Protestantism might have found a common base and erected a much broader ecumenical church out of the evangelical movement. But the forces of particularism in the nineteenth century were too strong, and gradually the Sunday school movement divided into the different denominational organizations. By 1860 the trend was clear.

The existence within the churches of a more or less vigorous school system which traditional ecclesiastical forces could not completely control meant that there was a continual demand upon the particularistic to deal with the broad. Long before there were many other significant ecumenical forces, the irritation kept alive in many churches by a Sunday school movement which had come to represent a broader Protestantism was acting to prevent the establishment of high-walled enclaves within Protestant denominations. However eagerly the church leaders tried to make of the Sunday school a denominational nurturing agency, it remained difficult to get the Sunday school to produce persons who were more narrowly denominational than broadly Christian.

The particularistic denominational training in seminaries and colleges and in ministerial teaching continued to have alongside it this more general Christian training dependent upon a Bible curriculum and untheologically trained lay teachers. Through these continuing extra-church organizational channels successive generations of lay leaders as well as teachers and pupils of the Sunday schools were made aware of dimensions of Christian experience broader than just the denominational or local church ones.

In the same way, the inertia of such a massive force, institutionalized independently, with its simplistic system of study and thought, contributed to American Christianity's failure to produce as highly sophisticated and relevant a theology as might otherwise have been the case during the past century. The effect of that broad ecumenical influence through the Sunday school has never been fully studied or appreciated, but by 1860 the framework for it had been formed.

In the process of formation, what was the understanding of the church held by those involved in the Sunday school movement? The shift to voluntarism during the period was perhaps doing something far more than changing the forms of church life. The very definition of the church was at stake. In the discussion at the 1837 Presbyterian General Assembly one of the commissioners was quoted as saying:

> Nor is it necessary that the work should be done by the church, in her ecclesiastical organization, in order to its being done *by the church,* and in a manner acceptable to God. What is the church, but the collective body of Christ's disciples? And what are the conscience and faith of the church, but the conscience and faith of her individual members? What then are the duties of the church, but the duties of the individuals who constitute it?[61]

By offering a parallel, quasi-ecclesiastical structure and outlet for Christian energies, the Sunday school movement complicated the search for a definition of the nature of the church in American Christianity.

Furthermore, although the strategy commitment of Protestant churches to the dual pattern perhaps weakened them as denominations, in the process they contributed to the establishment of a societal religion which has effectively helped the nation grow.[62] Along with other benevolent societies, the Sunday school contributed to what Winthrop Hudson calls "the greatest achievement of the free churches in 'the great century' —the placing of a distinctly Christian stamp upon an entire culture." [63]

In that context the Sunday school stood between the public school and the denominational church and kept them related. The Sunday school movement, even in 1860, furnished one of the instruments by which denominationalism was transcended and challenged and by which the public schools were kept aware of religious forces beyond their common faith. Standing thus midway, the Sunday school faced the severe problem of defining itself primarily by means of negative or derivative categories: as adjunct to the public school, as adjunct to the church in its denominational forms. The serious problem of definition underlay the difficult strategy decisions involved for the society and for the church with regard to education. During the National Period (1789-1860) working strategy decisions were made in both directions. The society accepted and supported the dual system of education, except for the then-insignificant Roman Catholic parochial school system. The church embraced the Sunday school and tried to fit it into traditional structures of church life and education, with only partial success.

But the problem of definition did not keep the instrument from working with signal effectiveness, for the ensuing half century was to see the American Sunday school burgeon into a religious educational phenomenon such as the world had never seen. Expanded into a world program, it was to influence the religious educational patterns of countries that had never seen the conditions out of which it had grown in England and America. And in America it was to continue to influence successive generations of Christians according to the particular emphases it included in its teaching.

Thus did the American Sunday school develop between 1789 and 1860, an educational and ecclesiastical hybrid. As such, it reflected some of the greater movements of societal and religious forces at work in the formative period of the nation's history and in turn contributed to them. Perhaps its major contribution to the educational strategy of the church in America has been its ambiguous nature as agency for church teaching, for this very ambiguity has continued to make it a bridge between church as previously conceived and church as it has been emerging in this society.

In such ways has the Sunday school helped the nation and

the church develop their educational systems. Investigation of the development of the Sunday school therefore contributes to greater understanding of the strategy decisions now being faced in the American society and in the church.

NOTES

PREFACE

1. Two recent historiographical essays point out the trends: William A. Clebsch, "A New Historiography of American Religion," *Historical Magazine of the Protestant Episcopal Church*, XXXII, No. 3 (September, 1963), 225-58; and Lawrence A. Cremin, *The Wonderful World of E. P. Cubberley* (New York: Teachers College Press, Columbia University, 1965). Both have helpful bibliographies.

PROLOGUE

1. For further treatment of the early beginnings, see G. P. Albaugh, "Sunday School Movement in the United States," in *An Encyclopedia of Religion,* ed. Vergilius Ferm (New York: The Philosophical Society, 1945), pp. 744-49. Other histories of the Sunday school useful in this study were as follows: James H. Blodgett, "Sunday Schools," in *Report of the Commissioner of Education for the Year 1896-97,* (Washington: Government Printing Office, 1898), I, 349-425; Clifton H. Brewer, *Early Episcopal Sunday Schools (1814-1865),* (Milwaukee: Morehouse Publishing Co., 1933); Clifton H. Brewer, *A History of Religious Education in The Episcopal Church Till 1835* (New Haven: Yale University Press, 1924); Marianna C. Brown, *Sunday-School Movements in America* (New York: Fleming H. Revell Co., 1901); Henry F. Cope, *The Evolution of the Sunday School* (Boston: Pilgrim Press, 1911); William Ewing, *The Sunday-School Century Containing a History of the Congregational Sunday-School and Publishing Society* (Boston: Pilgrim Press, 1918); Oscar S. Michael, *The Sunday-School in the Development of the American Church* (Milwaukee: The Young Churchman Co., 1904); Edwin Wilbur Rice, *The Sunday-School Movement and the American Sunday-School Union* (2d ed.; Philadelphia: The Union Press, 1917); Edwin Wilbur Rice, "Sunday-Schools," in *The New Schaff-Herzog Encyclopedia of Religious Knowledge* (New York and London: Funk & Wagnalls Co., 1911), XI, 151-65; George Stewart, *A His-*

tory of Religious Education in Connecticut to the Middle of the Nineteenth Century (New Haven: Yale University Press, 1924); Henry Clay Trumbull, *The Sunday-School; Its Origin, Mission, Methods, and Auxiliaries* (Philadelphia: John D. Wattles, Publisher, 1893); and Addie Grace Wardle, *History of the Sunday School Movement in the Methodist Episcopal Church* (New York: The Methodist Book Concern, 1918).

2. The standard history of the ASSU is Rice, *The Sunday-School Movement and the American Sunday-School Union, ibid.*

3. *Sixth Annual Report*, 1830, p. 4. (Unless otherwise specified, Annual Reports cited throughout are those of the ASSU.)

4. Publication statistics of the Sunday school societies show their part in the expansion of the publishing business in America during the second quarter of the century. They also reflect the early predominance of the ASSU and its later decline as sales increased for the denominational organizations.

CHAPTER 1

1. "Sunday Schools and the American Sunday-School Union," *American Journal of Education,* XV (1865), 720.

2. Mary G. Jones, *The Charity School Movement: A Study of Eighteenth Century Puritanism in Action* (Cambridge: The University Press, 1938), p. 346. Placing Robert Raikes in historical context, this book is indispensable for understanding the origins of the modern Sunday school.

3. In addition to the records cited in the bibliography, George W. Bethune, *Memoirs of Mrs. Joanna Bethune* (New York: Harper & Bros., 1863), describes the life of one of the pioneers of these city Sunday schools.

4. *Report of the Union Committee of the Sunday Schools of the Three Baptist Societies in Boston,* October 29, 1817, p. 5.

5. B. Paxson Drury, *A Fruitful Life: A Narrative of the Experiences and Missionary Labors of Stephen Paxson* (Philadelphia: The American Sunday School Union, 1882). Two other colorful personal accounts of Sunday school missionary activity are the following: Joseph H. McCullagh, *"The Sunday-School Man of the South." A Sketch of the Life and Labors of the Rev. John Mc-Cullagh* (Philadelphia: The American Sunday School Union, 1889); and B. W. Chidlaw, *The Story of My Life* (Philadelphia: Wm. H. Hirst, 1890).

6. *Annual Report*, 1831, pp. 41-42.

7. Particularly helpful for this study, from the extensive bibliography on the development of public education in America in Lawrence A. Cremin, *The Wonderful World of E. P. Cubberley* (New York: Teachers College Press, Columbia University, 1965), were

such studies as the following: Bernard Bailyn, *Education in the Forming of American Society* (Chapel Hill, N. C.: University of North Carolina Press, 1960); Bailyn claims that the "major axles" of society upon which formal education depends were shifting by the end of the colonial period. The standard history is Elwood P. Cubberley, *Public Education in the United States* (1919) (rev. and enl. ed.; Cambridge: The Riverside Press, Houghton Mifflin Co., 1947). Lawrence A. Cremin, in *The American Common School, An Historic Conception* (New York: Teachers College Press, Columbia University, 1951), studies carefully the rise of common schools. Among the helpful state histories are the following: Nelson R. Burr, *Education in New Jersey 1630-1871* (Princeton, N. J.: Princeton University Press, 1942); William A. Maddox, *The Free School Idea in Virginia Before the Civil War: A Phase of Political and Social Evolution* (New York: Teachers College Press, Columbia University, 1918); Joseph J. McCadden, *Education in Pennsylvania 1801-1835 and Its Debt to Roberts Vaux* (Philadelphia: University of Pennsylvania Press, 1937); and the older James P. Wickersham, *A History of Education in Pennsylvania, Private and Public, Elementary and Higher, From the Time the Swedes Settled on the Delaware to the Present Day* (Lancaster, Pa.: Inquirer Publishing Co., 1886). More recent, fresh interpretations include Rush Welter, *Popular Education and Democratic Thought in America* (New York: Columbia University Press, 1962); and Solon T. Kimball and James E. McClellan, *Education and the New America* (New York: Random House, 1962).

8. *The American Journal of Education and College Review*, eds. Absalom Peters and Henry Barnard, (June, 1856), I, No. VI, 603.

9. See Evarts B. Greene, "A Puritan Counter-Reformation," reprinted from the *Proceedings of the American Antiquarian Society for April, 1932* (Worcester, Mass.: Published by the Society, 1933), pp. 25 ff.

10. H. Shelton Smith, Robert T. Handy, and Lefferts A. Loetscher, *American Christianity, An Historical Interpretation With Representative Documents* (New York: Charles Scribner's Sons, 1963), II, 8, 16.

11. *Annual Report*, 1856, p. 24. See also the quote from the *American Journal of Education* cited by Note 1 of this chapter.

12. Cubberley, *op. cit.*, pp. 121 ff.

13. *American Journal of Education*, XV, *op. cit.*

14. Edward Twisleton, *Evidence as to the Religious Working of the Common Schools in the State of Massachusetts, with a Preface by The Hon. Edward Twisleton, Late Chief Commissioner of Poor Laws in Ireland* (2d ed.; London: James Ridgway, 1854), pp. 5, 6. Among other contemporaries who confirmed the general acceptance of the "dual pattern" were the following: William O.

Bourne, *History of the Public School Society of the City of New York* (New York: William Wood & Co., 1870); Elisha R. Potter, *Reports and Documents Upon Public Schools and Education in the State of Rhode Island* (Providence: Knowles, Anthony & Co., Printers, 1855); P. A. Siljestrom, *Educational Institutions of the United States, Their Character and Organization,* trans. Frederick Rowan (London: John Chapman, 1853); Calvin E. Stowe, *The Religious Element in Education* (Boston: William D. Ticknor & Co., 1844); and Hugh S. Tremenheere, *Notes on Public Subjects, Made During a Tour in the United States and in Canada* (London: John Murray, 1852).

15. Benjamin O. Peers, *American Education: Or Strictures on the Nature, Necessity, and Practicability of a System of National Education, Suited to the United States* (New York: John S. Taylor, 1838), p. 280.

16. For instance, Horace Bushnell, "Christianity and Common Schools," reprinted from the *Connecticut Common School Journal* in *The Common School Journal,* Boston, II (1840), 57-60; and Nahum Gale, "The True Theory of Public Schools: Illustrated by the Constitution and Laws of Massachusetts," *The American Journal of Education and College Review,* II (July-December, 1856), 19-31.

17. Quoted in William K. Dunn, *What Happened to Religious Education? The Decline of Religious Teaching in the Public Elementary School 1776-1861* (Baltimore: The Johns Hopkins Press, 1958), p. 65.

18. *Ibid.,* p. 139.

19. Twisleton, *op. cit.,* p. 75. The correspondent was Barnas Sears, successor to Horace Mann as Secretary of the Massachusetts Board of Education.

20. Stowe, *op. cit.,* p. 32. The anti-Catholic reference indicates the strong feelings in this period of American nativism. Contemporary documents show this feeling, along with sectarian hostilities, mixed into the ambivalent Protestant support for common schools. Helpful resources include the following: Contemporary accounts— Stephen Colwell, *The Position of Christianity in the United States, in Its Relations With Our Political Institutions, and Specially With Reference to Religious Instruction in the Public Schools* (Philadelphia: Lippincott, Grambo, & Co., 1854); Philip Schaff, *America: A Sketch of Its Political, Social, and Religious Character,* ed. Perry Miller (Cambridge, Mass.: Harvard University Press, 1961); Philip Schaff, *Church and State in the United States or The American Idea of Religious Liberty and Its Practical Effects with Official Documents* (New York: G. P. Putnam's Sons, 1888); and Matthew Hale Smith, *The Bible, the Rod, and Religion, in Common Schools* (Boston, 1847). Roman Catholic analyses—Dunn,

op. cit.; Francis X. Curran, *The Churches and the Schools: American Protestantism and Popular Elementary Education* (Chicago: Loyola University Press, 1954); and Neil G. McCluskey, *Public Schools and Moral Education* (New York: Columbia University Press, 1958). General studies—Raymond B. Culver, *Horace Mann and Religion in the Massachusetts Public Schools* (New Haven, Conn.: Yale University Press, 1929); Conrad H. Moehlman, *School and Church: The American Way: An Historical Approach to the Problem of Religious Instruction in Public Education* (New York: Harper & Bros., 1944); Sherman M. Smith, *The Relation of the State to Religious Education in Massachusetts* (Syracuse, N. Y.: Syracuse University Book Store, 1926); George M. Stephenson, *The Puritan Heritage* (New York: The Macmillan Co., 1952); and Anson Phelps Stokes, *Church and State in the United States,* (3 vols.; New York: Harper & Bros., 1950). The fact that there was vigorous anti-Catholic feeling and undoubtedly some political cynicism regarding denominational support of public schools need not rule out other powerful motivations. As Henry F. May said in a review of Curran's book (cited earlier in this note) in the *Mississippi Valley Historical Review,* XLI, No. 3 (December, 1954), 516: "American Protestants of the nineteenth century were republicans as well as Christians, and they identified popular education both with true religion and with proper government. For many, though not for all, the important thing was to teach the children to read. Even in the absence of doctrinal instruction it was unthinkable that in Christian America education could fail to turn out good Protestants. Only to the most rigidly orthodox was the cause of the common school a surrender of religion in the 1840's." Despite the various approaches to this complex historical question, the general expectation of Protestants that common schools teach basic religion or morality seems clear.

21. Sherman M. Smith, *ibid.,* p. 106.
22. Foreword to *McGuffey's Fifth Eclectic Reader, 1879 Edition* (New York: The New American Library of World Literature, Inc., 1962), p. vii. Richard D. Mosier makes the same point in *Making the American Mind: Social and Moral Ideas in the McGuffey Readers* (New York: King's Crown Press, 1947), p. 19, as does Ruth M. Elson in "American Schoolbooks and 'Culture' in the Nineteenth Century," *Mississippi Valley Historical Review,* XLVI, No. 3 (December, 1959), 434.
23. In *The American Common School, An Historic Conception, op. cit.,* pp. 67 ff., Cremin discusses more fully these two aspects of "education for moral adequacy."
24. Frank G. Lankard, *A History of the American Sunday School Curriculum* (New York: Abingdon Press, 1927), Chapter IX.
25. A. D. Mayo, "The American Common Schools in the Southern

States During the First Half Century of the Republic, 1790-1840,"
in *Report of the Commissioner of Education for the Year 1895-
96,* (Washington: Government Printing Office, 1897), I, 279.
Mayo's paragraph reads: "Probably the only American state that
has taken the original Sunday school idea of Robert Raikes into its
educational system is Delaware. In 1821 the state provided that
every school held on the Sabbath Day for the instruction of white
children should be subsidized at the rate of twenty cents per capita.
In 1829 there were 19 schools of this sort receiving the aggregate
sum of $224.00. This feature is still retained in the common-
school system of the state, and each of its counties receives annu-
ally $500.00 for the maintenance of Sunday schools. Here is per-
petuated the old English idea of subsidizing the schools of the
different religious sects."

26. McCluskey, *op. cit.,* p. 261, traces the search for effective moral
instruction through the work of Horace Mann, William Torrey
Harris and John Dewey and concludes that "after many decades
of experimenting, the problem of moral education in the common
public school is more defiant of solution than ever—is, in fact, in-
soluble."

27. Reply to an address, November 29, 1841, in *The Complete Works
of the Most Rev. John Hughes, D. D., Archbishop of New York,*
ed. Lawrence Kehoe, (New York: The American News Co.,
1864), I, 126.

28. Sidney E. Mead, *The Lively Experiment: The Shaping of Christianity in America* (New York: Harper & Row, 1963), p. 68.

29. Ray A. Billington popularized the term in *The Protestant Crusade,
1800-1860* (New York: Holt, Rinehart & Winston, 1952).

30. Winthrop S. Hudson, *The Great Tradition of the American
Churches* (New York: Harper & Row, 1963), p. 108. Dunn, *op.
cit.,* and Curran, *op. cit.,* also make this point.

31. Hudson, *ibid.,* p. 109.

32. James Hastings Nichols, "Religion and Education in a Free Society," in *Religion in America,* ed. John Cogley (New York: The
World Publishing Co., 1958), pp. 151, 149.

CHAPTER 2

1. Frederick A. Packard, *Popular Sketch of the Rise and Progress of
Sunday-Schools in the United States* (Philadelphia: The American
Sunday School Union, n.d. [c. 1845], p. 19.

2. *Ibid.,* p. 16.

3. *A Brief History of the Mass. [sic] Sabbath School Society, and of
the Rise and Progress of Sabbath Schools in the Orthodox Congregational Denomination in Massachusetts* (Boston: Mass. Sabbath
School Society, 1850), p. 29.

4. Clifton H. Brewer, *Early Episcopal Sunday Schools (1814-1865)*, (Milwaukee: Morehouse Publishing Co., 1933), p. 88.
5. Andrew Reed and James Matheson, *A Narrative of the Visit to the American Churches, by the Deputation From the Congregational Union of England and Wales* (London: Jackson & Walford, 1835), p. 389; and others, for instance, Archibald Alexander, in "The Pastoral Office," sermon to alumni of Princeton Seminary, 1834 (Philadelphia: Henry Perkins, 1834).
6. See, for instance, Archibald Alexander, "The Duty of Catechetical Instruction" (Philadelphia: Presbyterian Board of Publication, 1836).
7. "Bishop Doane's Contribution," in *Memorial Papers. The Memorial: with Circular and Questions of the Episcopal Commission. . . .* with an introduction by Rt. Rev. Alonzo Potter (Philadelphia: E. H. Butler & Co., 1857), p. 88.
8. See, for instance, the summary of a committee report to the 1841 General Convention of the Protestant Episcopal Church, in Oscar S. Michael, *The Sunday-School in the Development of the American Church* (Milwaukee: The Young Churchman Co., 1904), p. 187.
9. William Ellery Channing, "The Sunday School. A Discourse Pronounced Before the Sunday School Society," *The Christian Examiner,* LXXIX (March, 1837), 75.
10. Sidney E. Mead describes the shift in "The Rise of the Evangelical Conception of the Ministry in America: 1607-1850," in *The Ministry in Historical Perspectives,* eds. H. R. Niebuhr and D. D. Williams (New York: Harper & Bros., 1956), pp. 207-49. This section explores certain educational implications of Mead's essay.
11. Michael, *op. cit.,* differentiates the Sunday school from catechetical, confirmation, and day-school instruction, and criticizes H. Clay Trumbull's Beecher Lectures of 1888, *The Sunday-School; Its Origin, Mission, Methods, and Auxiliaries* (Philadelphia: John D. Wattles, Publisher, 1893), for ignoring the distinctions.
12. Trumbull, *ibid.,* Chapter IV, raised serious questions about the nostalgia for "the good old days" of family worship.
13. J. E. K. Henshaw, "The Usefulness of Sunday-Schools," sermon preached at Philadelphia, May 20, 1833, from *Sermons Delivered at the Request of the American Sunday-School Union, at the Anniversaries of the Society* (Philadelphia: The American Sunday School Union, n.d.), p. 11.
14. *Annual Report,* 1858, pp. 43-44.
15. J. W. [sic], "Doctrinal Instruction in Sunday Schools," *The Christian Examiner and Religious Miscellany,* XLIV (January, 1848), 33.
16. Reed and Matheson, *op. cit.,* pp. 387-89.
17. See William A. Hallock, *"Light and Love." A Sketch of the Life*

and Labors of the Rev. Justin Edwards, D. D. the Evangelical Pastor; the Advocate of Temperance, the Sabbath, and the Bible (New York: American Tract Society, 1855), pp. 150 ff.

18. *The American Bible Class Society, Second Annual Report*, presented in Philadelphia, May 26, 1829 (Williamsport, 1830), p. 6.

19. Packard, *op. cit.*, pp. 44, 45. Sunday school and adult Bible classes in New England churches are described in letters written to the Sabbath School and Bible Class Association of Andover Theological Seminary in 1829, quoted in Asa Bullard, *Fifty Years with the Sabbath Schools* (Boston: Lockwood, Brooks, & Co., 1876), pp. 54 ff., and in the chapter on adult classes, pp. 180-86. Other reports are found in *The American Sunday School Magazine* (February, 1825; March and August, 1829) and *The Biblical Repertory and Theological Review* (April, 1830).

20. *American Sunday School Magazine* (August, 1829), p. 231.

21. See discussion of the problem later in this chapter in the third paragraph of the section entitled "The Problem of Leadership."

22. C. Howard Hopkins, *History of the Y. M. C. A. in North America* (New York: Association Press, 1951), p. 16 and *passim*.

23. Francis P. Cassidy, "Catholic Education in the Third Plenary Council of Baltimore," *The Catholic Historical Review*, XXXIV, No. 3 (October, 1948), 257.

24. *Ibid.*, No. 4 (January, 1949), 434. Cassidy's articles make it clear that some Catholic church leaders objected strongly to the final commitment to parochial schools. There were other alternatives. Orestes A. Brownson, convert to Catholicism, maintained in two intriguing articles that parochial schools were not essential to the preservation of the Catholic church in America: "School and Education," *Brownson's Quarterly Review*, (July, 1854) in *The Works of Orestes A. Brownson* (Detroit: Thorndike Nourse, Publisher, 1884), X, 564-84; and "Public and Parochial Schools," *Brownson's Quarterly Review* (July, 1859) in *The Works of Orestes A. Brownson, ibid.*, XII, 200-16.

25. The standard but dated history of Catholic education in the United States is James A. Burns, *The Growth and Development of the Catholic School System in the United States* (New York: Benziger, 1912). Good examples of newer interpretations are found in Neil G. McCluskey, *The Catholic Viewpoint on Education* (Garden City, N. Y.: Hanover House, 1959); and *Catholic Education in America, A Documentary History*, ed. Neil G. McCluskey (New York: Teachers College Press, Columbia University, 1964). Other recent studies indicate considerable re-evaluation of the traditional viewpoint, as in Mary P. Ryan, *Are Parochial Schools the Answer?: Catholic Education in the Light of the Council* (New York: Holt, Rinehart & Winston, 1963).

26. Lewis J. Sherrill, *Presbyterian Parochial Schools 1846-1870* (New

Haven, Conn.: Yale University Press, 1932). Sherrill's more detailed dissertation is available at Sterling Library of Yale University. His conclusions about the Sunday school confirm those stated above.

27. *Ibid.*, p. 181.
28. *Ibid.*, pp. 179, 180, 181.
29. In recent years American higher education has received much careful study. One major earlier work, stressing sectarian competition, is D. G. Tewksbury, *The Founding of American Colleges and Universities before the Civil War, with Particular Reference to the Religious Influences Bearing on the College Movement* (New York: Teachers College Press, Columbia University, 1932). Recent works include the following: *The Colleges and the Public, 1787-1862,* ed. Theodore R. Crane (New York: Teachers College Press, Columbia University, 1963); Frederick Rudolph, *The American College and University: A History* (New York: Alfred A. Knopf, Inc., 1962); and several works of Richard Hofstadter and others, of which *The Development and Scope of Higher Education in the United States* (New York: Columbia University Press, 1952) and *American Higher Education: A Documentary History* (2 vols.; Chicago: University of Chicago Press, 1961) are important. Crane's suggestive essay includes a long and helpful bibliographical footnote on p. 2.
30. From *Biblical Reportory and Princeton Review,* IX (1837), quoted in H. Shelton Smith, Robert T. Handy, and Lefferts A. Loetscher, *American Christianity, An Historical Interpretation With Representative Documents* (New York: Charles Scribner's Sons, 1963), II, pp. 90-91.
31. Again the analysis draws implications from Mead's essay in Niebuhr and Williams, *op. cit.*
32. *Annual Report,* 1841, p. 25.
33. "The Happy Adaptation of the Sabbath School System to the Peculiar Wants of Our Age and Country. A Sermon, preached at the request of the Board of Managers of the American Sunday-School Union," (Philadelphia, May 20, 1839), in *Sermons Delivered at the Request of the American Sunday-School Union . . . , op. cit.*, p. 7.
34. *Annual Report,* 1842, p. 40.
35. *Annual Report,* 1841, *op. cit.*, pp. 22-23.
36. "Hints for the Formation of Sunday Schools," *The American Sunday School Teachers' Magazine, and Journal of Education,* I (February, 1824), 69.
37. B. W. Chidlaw, *The Story of My Life* (Philadelphia: Wm. H. Hirst, 1890), p. 128.
38. *The American Sunday School Teachers' Magazine, and Journal of Education,* I (March, 1824), 111. It is difficult to get a clear pic-

ture of actual classroom procedures around 1824; possibly this was quite typical.

39. The Lancasterian or Monitorial School experiments no doubt influenced these developments.

40. Stephen H. Tyng, *Forty Years' Experience in Sunday-Schools* (New York: Sheldon & Co., 1863), p. 23.

41. Michael, *op. cit.,* p. 140.

42. Bullard, *op. cit.,* p. 102.

43. Alexander, "The Pastoral Office," *op. cit.,* pp. 17-18.

44. *Memorial Papers, The Memorial . . . , op. cit.,* pp. 93-94.

45. The evidence of this study would support the brief reference of Smith, Handy, and Loetscher, *op. cit.,* p. 73, to this tension, involving the danger of loss not only of clerical power, but also of ecclesiastical and theological tradition. Charles I. Foster, *An Errand of Mercy* (Chapel Hill, N. C.: University of North Carolina Press, 1960), gives a stimulating analysis of the relationship of American denominations to the Evangelical United Front, as he calls it. Because of the importance of the benevolent societies in understanding the religious history of the nineteenth century, they have received much recent scholarly attention. In addition to Foster, there are other major interpretations which include extensive bibliographies of studies of the particular movements and their leaders, such as the following, which were particularly useful for this study: Timothy L. Smith, *Revivalism and Social Reform in Mid-Nineteenth Century America* (New York: Abingdon Press, 1957); Charles C. Cole, Jr., *The Social Ideas of the Northern Evangelists 1826-1860* (New York: Columbia University Press, 1954); Gilbert H. Barnes, *The Antislavery Impulse 1830-1844* (New York: D. Appleton-Century Co., 1933); John R. Bodo, *The Protestant Clergy and Public Issues 1812-1848* (Princeton, N. J.: Princeton University Press, 1954); Clifford S. Griffin, *Their Brothers' Keepers; Moral Stewardship in the United States, 1800-1865* (New Brunswick, N. J.: Rutgers University Press, 1960); James F. Maclear, "'The True American Union' of Church and State: The Reconstruction of the Theocratic Tradition," *Church History*, XXVIII, No. 1 (March, 1959), 41-62; and Ray A. Billington, *The Protestant Crusade, 1800-1860* (New York: Holt, Rinehart, & Winston, 1952).

46. Edwin Wilbur Rice, *The Sunday-School Movement and the American Sunday School Union* (2d ed.; Philadelphia: The Union Press, 1917), p. 54.

47. Winthrop S. Hudson describes the dramatic change in Lyman Beecher in "Lyman Beecher's Great Discovery," Chapter IV in *The Great Tradition of the American Churches* (New York: Harper & Row, 1963), pp. 63-79.

48. Particularly Billington and Griffin, but see also the other studies cited in Note 45.
49. Gaylord P. Albaugh, "Antimissionary Movement," *Twentieth Century Encyclopedia of Religious Knowledge* (Grand Rapids, Mich.: Baker Book House, 1955), p. 48.
50. Foster, *op. cit.*, p. 122.
51. *Annual Report*, 1833, p. 14.
52. Rice, *op. cit.*, p. 84. H. Richard Niebuhr discusses the nature of American Protestantism as primarily movement and secondarily order, in "The Protestant Movement and Democracy in the United States," in *The Shaping of American Religion*, eds. James Ward Smith and A. Leland Jamison (Princeton, N. J.: Princeton University Press, 1961), pp. 20-71.
53. Analyses like that of Foster, *op. cit.*, which speak of a "collapse of the united front" underestimate the considerable lasting activity and effect of certain organized parts of the benevolent society movement, in particular the American Bible Society and, to a lesser extent, the ASSU.
54. *Annual Report*, 1857, p. viii.
55. See Perry Miller, "From the Covenant to the Revival," in Smith and Jamison, *op. cit.*, pp. 360-61.
56. *Annual Report*, 1847, p. 17.
57. *Annual Report*, 1844, p. 57.
58. James Hastings Nichols, "Religion and Education in a Free Society," in *Religion in America*, ed. John Cogley (New York: The World Publishing Co., 1958), p. 152.
59. Sidney E. Mead, *The Lively Experiment: The Shaping of Christianity in America* (New York: Harper & Row, 1963), pp. 139-40.
60. Smith, Handy, and Loetscher, *op. cit.*, pp. 67-68. Also the Methodists and the Baptists (1845).
61. Quoted in Foster, *op. cit.*, p. 271, from *A Plea for Voluntary Societies*, by a Member of the General Assembly (New York, 1837), p. 23.
62. J. Paul Williams, *What Americans Believe and How They Worship*, (rev. ed.; New York: Harper & Row, 1962), p. 140 and *passim*.
63. Hudson, *op. cit.*, p. 101.

SELECTED BIBLIOGRAPHY

In addition to the bibliographical references in the NOTES, the following have provided the major resource material for the interpretation of the Sunday school in this study.

I. ANNUAL REPORTS

The American Sunday School Union, I-XXXVI (1825-60 [except 1859]).
Boston Sabbath School Union, 1-12 (1830-41).
The Boston Society for the Moral and Religious Instruction of the Poor, I-XIV (1817-30).
Boston Sunday School Society [*Unitarian*], 1829, 1839, 1842, 1850, and 1852.
General Protestant Episcopal Sunday School Union, 1828, 1829, 1832, 1834-38, 1851, and 1854.
General Protestant Episcopal Sunday School Union, Executive Committee of the Board of Managers, 1828, 1829, 1832, 1834, 1836-38, 1847, 1851, and 1854.
General Protestant Episcopal Sunday School Union, Triennial Reports, 1835, 1838, 1847, and 1859.
Massachusetts General Association, Report of the, in *New England Puritan,* [July ?] 12, 1844.
Massachusetts Sabbath School Society, 1-17, 21-24 (1833-1849, 1853-1856).
Methodist Episcopal Church: Sunday School Union of the, 1845, 1847, 1848, 1850-56, 1858, and 1859.
New York Female Union Society for the Promotion of Sabbath Schools, Third and Fifth (1819 and 1821).
New York Protestant Episcopal Sunday School Society. First (1817).
New York Sunday School Union Society, 1, 2, 3, 4, and 5 (1817, 1818, 1820, and 1821).
Philadelphia Sunday and Adult School Union, Fourth (1821).
Protestant Reformed Dutch Church, Report of the Board of Managers of the General Synod's Sabbath-School Union, Tenth (1849).

II. PERIODICALS

American Journal of Education (Boston), I-IV (1826-30).
American Journal of Education, I-XXII (1855-71).
The American Sunday School Magazine, I, II, IV-VI (1824, 1825, 1827-29).
The American Sunday School Teacher's Magazine, and Journal of Education, I (1823-24).
The Common School Journal, I-X (1839-48).
Journal of Christian Education, and Family and Sunday-School Visiter [*sic*], I-IV (1839-42).

III. MISCELLANEOUS

ALEXANDER, JAMES W. *The American Sunday-School and Its Adjuncts.* Philadelphia: The American Sunday School Union, 1856. 342 pp.

"An Article on the American Sunday-School Union," *Biblical Repertory and Theological Review* (Philadelphia), (April, 1830).

BOARDMAN, HENRY A. *Not "This" or "That," but "This" and "That."* Philadelphia: March 5, 1858.

Historical Sketch of the American Sunday-School Union and of its Contributions to Popular Education in the United States. Philadelphia: The American Sunday School Union, n.d. [1864 ?]. 45 pp.

HOBART, JOHN HENRY. "The Beneficial Effects of Sunday Schools Considered. . . ." New York, 1817.

PACKARD, FREDERICK A. "Letters on the Design and Importance of the Agency of the American Sunday-School Union in New England." Philadelphia, 1838.

Presbyterian Church in the United States of America. *A Collection of the Acts, Deliverances, and Testimonies of the Supreme Judicatory of the Presbyterian Church from its Origin in America to the Present Time.* Compiled by SAMUEL J. BAIRD. Philadelphia, 1856. [*Old School*].

————. *A New Digest of the Acts and Deliverances of the General Assembly of the. . . .* Compiled by the Order and Authority of the General Assembly, by WILLIAM E. MOORE. Philadelphia, 1861. [*New School*].

————. *The Presbyterian Digest: A Compend of the Acts and Deliverances of the General Assembly of the. . . .* Compiled by WILLIAM E. MOORE. Philadelphia, 1873.

————, Board of Education. *Report of the . . . on Parochial Schools.* Philadelphia, 1847. 32 pp.

Protestant Reformed Dutch Church. *Constitution and By-Laws of the*

Board of Managers of the General Synod's Sabbath School Union of the. . . . New York, 1848. 16 pp.

TYNG, STEPHEN H. "The American Sunday-School Union and the 'Union Principle.'" In reply to A. in *The Episcopal Recorder* (New York), 1855. 50 pp.

WILBUR, HERVEY. "A Discourse on the Religious Education of Youth, Delivered at Homer [New York], on the Evening Previous to the Meeting of Synod, the eleventh of October, 1814." 2d ed. Boston, 1814. 16 pp.